THE POEM
OF
THE MIND

PHOTOGRAPH COURTESY OF THE MUSEUM OF MODERN ART

Joan Miró, Self Portrait, 1937-38. Collection, James Thrall Soby

THE POEM OF THE MIND

Essays on Poetry / English and American

LOUIS L. MARTZ

New York / Oxford University Press / 1966

So, in me, come flinging
Forms, flames, and the flakes of flames.

WALLACE STEVENS

Library of Congress Catalogue Card Number: 66–14480

PRINTED IN THE UNITED STATES OF AMERICA

For E.M.M.

WHO WATCHED THESE GROW

CONTENTS

PREFACE

Miró's self portrait, with its haunting combination of discipline and fantasy, its sternly molded features and ascending flames, its realistic lines sweeping upward from a dark ground through mysterious floating shapes toward an inner incandescence, has come more and more to seem an appropriate image of this book's essential themes. For most of these essays deal with poetry of the interior life, where the mind, acutely aware of an outer world of drifting, unstable forms, finds within itself the power to create coherence and significance. As Wallace Stevens (in many ways the presiding genius of this book) says, it seems that in such poetry

> the mind
> Turns to its own figurations and declares,
> *"This image, this love, I compose myself*
> *Of these. In these I come forth outwardly."*

The essays have been selected and arranged with the aim of suggesting an underlying continuity when they are read in the present sequence. But a reading of the first and the last essays together will suggest the associative continuity that I have in mind. The essays were, of course, composed on separate occasions and, with one exception, they have been published previously, in one form or another. Nevertheless, a relationship seemed to arise from the way in which the essays reflect a preoccupation with the poetry of the introspective self—a preoccupation shown by the repetition of certain themes and quotations. Most of these repetitions have been retained here, since they seemed essential to a given essay and might at the same time serve to link the essays informally. Although one of the recurrent themes is a concern with the nature of meditative poetry, there is no intention of grouping all these poets under a single term; they are too various.

The one essay previously (for the most part) unpublished, "Whitman and Dickinson: Two Aspects of the Self," is designed to illuminate, by contrast, two different kinds of poetry, the prophetic and the meditative. This essay contains materials that have been presented in lectures on several occasions; it stands here largely as it was prepared for a Winston Churchill Lecture at the University of Bristol in 1963, except that in the latter part I have replaced an informal discussion with similar materials that have appeared in print as part of a review-article on Emily Dickinson's poetry. The two essays on another "prophetic" poet, William Carlos Williams, have undergone considerable revision. In the first of these, numerous titles and dates have been changed or added, and minor excisions and revisions of phrasing have been made here and there, but the essay remains substantially unchanged. The second essay on Williams has been thoroughly recast in order to remove some overlapping and to connect it more firmly with the preceding essay. The piece entitled "Meditative Action and 'The Metaphysick Style' " represents a considerable expansion of materials that first appeared in 1963 as an introduction to a collection of seventeenth-century poems; in this extensive revision I have tried to bring into focus certain issues concerning meditative poetry that are involved in some of the other essays. The remaining pieces stand substantially as they first appeared, with some excisions and some reworking of passages; here and there phrases and sentences have been added, but the only significant addition in these other pieces is a page in the middle of the essay on Eliot, concerning some relevant biographical matters that have recently come to light. As a matter of principle I have tried not to make any changes that affect the central point of view presented in the original essay.

L. L. M.

Saybrook College
Yale University
December 1965

ACKNOWLEDGMENTS

The essays have received previous publication as follows:

I. Published in *The Massachusetts Review*, 1 (1960), 326-42; copyright © 1960 by The Massachusetts Review, Inc.

II. Originally entitled "Donne and the Meditative Tradition," *Thought*, 34 (1959), 269-78; copyright © 1959 by Fordham University Press.

III. Originally, in shorter form, the Introduction to *The Meditative Poem: An Anthology of Seventeenth-Century Verse*, New York, Anchor Books, 1963; copyright © 1963 by Louis L. Martz; reprinted by permission of Doubleday & Company, Inc. This essay now incorporates materials from an essay on Donne's "Hymn to God my God, in my sicknesse" written for *Master Poems of the English Language*, ed. Oscar Williams, New York, Trident Press, 1966; copyright © 1966 by the Trident Press.

IV. Originally the Foreword to *The Poems of Edward Taylor*, ed. Donald E. Stanford, New Haven, Yale University Press, 1960; copyright © 1960 by Yale University Press, Inc.

V. Contains passages from a review-article dealing with Thomas Johnson's edition of Emily Dickinson's poetry: *University of Toronto Quarterly*, 26 (1957), 556-65; reprinted by permission of the publisher, University of Toronto Press.

VI. Published in *Sewanee Review*, 55 (1947), 126-47; copyright 1947 by the University of the South. Slightly expanded for inclusion in *T. S. Eliot: A Selected Critique*, ed. Leonard Unger, New York, Rinehart and Co., 1948; copyright 1948 by Leonard Unger.

VII. Published in *Poetry New York*, No. 4 (1951), 18-32; copyright 1951 by *Poetry New York*.

VIII. Originally entitled "The Unicorn in *Paterson:* William Carlos Williams," *Thought*, 35 (1960), 537-54; copyright © 1960 by Fordham University Press.

IX. Published in *Theodore Roethke: Essays on the Poetry*, ed. Arnold Stein, Seattle, University of Washington Press, 1965; copyright © 1965 by the University of Washington Press.

X. Originally entitled "The World of Wallace Stevens," in *Modern American Poetry, Focus Five*, ed. B. Rajan, London, Dennis Dobson Ltd.,

1950; all rights reserved. This essay of 1950 incorporates some passages from an earlier essay, "Wallace Stevens: The Romance of the Precise," *Yale Poetry Review*, No. 5 (1946), 13-20; copyright 1946 by *Yale Poetry Review*.

XI. Published in *The Yale Review*, 47 (1958), 517-36; and in *Literature and Belief: English Institute Essays*, ed. M. H. Abrams, New York, Columbia University Press, 1958; copyright © 1958 by Columbia University Press (previous copyright transferred by *Yale Review*).

I am grateful to all the periodicals, publishers, and copyright-holders named above for permission to reprint materials from the sources cited.

I am also grateful to the following for permission to quote:

The Clarendon Press, Oxford, for quotations from *The Poems of John Donne*, ed. Sir Herbert J. C. Grierson.

Harvard University Press for quotations from *The Poems of Emily Dickinson*, ed. Thomas H. Johnson, copyright 1951, 1955 by the President and Fellows of Harvard College. Little, Brown and Co. for two poems in *The Complete Poems of Emily Dickinson*, ed. Thomas H. Johnson: "It's easy to invent a Life," copyright 1929, © 1957 by Mary L. Hampson; and "To be alive—is Power," copyright 1914, 1942 by Martha Dickinson Bianchi.

Harcourt, Brace & World, Inc., and Faber & Faber Ltd. for quotations from T. S. Eliot, *Collected Poems, 1909-1962* and *Murder in the Cathedral*: specifically for lines from "Burnt Norton" in *Four Quartets*, copyright 1943 by T. S. Eliot, reprinted by permission; and for lines from *Murder in the Cathedral* by T. S. Eliot, copyright 1935 by Harcourt, Brace & World, Inc., copyright © 1963 by T. S. Eliot, reprinted by permission.

New Directions and Macgibbon & Kee Ltd. for quotations from *Paterson* by William Carlos Williams, copyright 1958 by William Carlos Williams, © 1963 by Florence Williams; from *Collected Earlier Poems of William Carlos Williams*, copyright 1938, 1951 by William Carlos Williams; from *Collected Later Poems of William Carlos Williams*, copyright 1944, © 1964 by William Carlos Williams; reprinted by permission of the publishers. New Directions for quotations from *In the American Grain*, copyright 1925 by James Laughlin, copyright 1933 by William Carlos Williams, reprinted by permission of the publisher.

New Directions and Mr. Arthur V. Moore, Mr. Pound's literary agent, for quotations from *The Cantos of Ezra Pound*, copyright 1934, 1937, 1940, 1948 by Ezra Pound, reprinted by permission of the publisher and Mr. Moore.

Doubleday & Company, Inc., for quotations from the poetry of Theodore Roethke, as follows: "The Longing," "Meditation at Oyster River," "Journey to the Interior," "The Far Field," "The Rose," "Otto," from *The*

Far Field by Theodore Roethke, copyright © 1958, 1959, 1960, 1961, 1962, 1963, 1964 by Beatrice Roethke; "Weed Puller," "Flower Dump," "Moss Gathering," "Child on Top of a Greenhouse," "Carnations," copyright 1946 by Editorial Publications, Inc.; "Root Cellar," copyright 1943 by Modern Poetry Association, Inc.; "The Return," copyright 1946 by Modern Poetry Association, Inc.; "Big Wind," copyright 1947 by The United Chapters of Phi Beta Kappa; "Old Florist," copyright © 1964 by Harper & Brothers; "A Field of Light," copyright 1948 by The Tiger's Eye; "The Adamant," copyright 1938 by Theodore Roethke; "Open House," "The Long Alley," copyright 1941 by Theodore Roethke; "The Minimal," copyright 1942 by Theodore Roethke; "Dolor," "The Lost Son," "The Shape of the Fire," copyright 1947 by Theodore Roethke; "Cuttings," "Orchids," "Transplanting," copyright 1948 by Theodore Roethke; "Frau Bauman, Frau Schmidt, and Frau Schwartze" (originally published in the *New Yorker*), copyright 1952 by Theodore Roethke; all from *Words for the Wind* by Theodore Roethke, reprinted by permission of Doubleday & Company, Inc.

Alfred A. Knopf, Inc., and Faber & Faber Ltd. for quotations from *Opus Posthumous* by Wallace Stevens, copyright © 1957 by Elsie Stevens and Holly Stevens; from *The Necessary Angel* by Wallace Stevens, copyright 1949, 1951 by Wallace Stevens; from *Collected Poems of Wallace Stevens,* copyright 1954 by Wallace Stevens; all reprinted by permission of the publishers: specifically, for "Nomad Exquisite," copyright 1923 and renewed 1951 by Wallace Stevens; "The Red Fern," copyright 1947 by Wallace Stevens; "The World as Meditation," copyright 1952 by Wallace Stevens; and Section III from "The Man with the Blue Guitar," copyright 1935, 1936 by Wallace Stevens; all reprinted from *Collected Poems of Wallace Stevens.*

I am grateful to the Museum of Modern Art for providing an excellent photograph by Soichi Sunami from which the frontispiece of the book has been made. And finally, I wish to thank Mr. James Thrall Soby for his generous permission to reproduce the self portrait of Miró that forms a part of his distinguished collection.

L. L. M.

THE POEM
OF
THE MIND

I

John Donne:
The Meditative Voice

SOME time ago, while reading in the poetry of Wallace Stevens, I came across two poems, side by side, that seemed to give an almost perfect definition of the poetry of John Donne, and indeed of a world-wide kind of poetry that I should like to call the meditative poem. It is the kind of poetry that, in Stevens' words,

> to find what will suffice,
> Destroys romantic tenements
> Of rose and ice. . .

If one thinks of the rose in the cheeks of every Petrarchan mistress, and of the equally inevitable ice in her heart, the lines may seem a perfect account of the impact of Donne upon English poetry, especially as Stevens concludes the first of these two poems, "Man and Bottle":

> The poem lashes more fiercely than the wind,
> As the mind, to find what will suffice, destroys
> Romantic tenements of rose and ice.

And then the companion-piece, "Of Modern Poetry," completes a definition of "The poem of the mind in the act of finding/What will suffice":

It has
To construct a new stage. It has to be on that stage
And, like an insatiable actor, slowly and
With meditation, speak words that in the ear,
In the delicatest ear of the mind, repeat,
Exactly, that which it wants to hear. . .

This actor, he adds, is "A metaphysician in the dark, twanging /An instrument, twanging a wiry string that gives/Sounds . . . wholly/Containing the mind." He is an actor who achieves, in the end, "The poem of the act of the mind."

In describing this kind of poetry, Stevens thoughtfully uses both the word *meditation* and the word *metaphysician,* thus allowing us to call this poetry either *metaphysical* or *meditative.* There is, I guess, no hope of discarding the worn term *metaphysical poetry* despite its vague and wandering applications; it is historically established; it serves to indicate certain qualities of style; and, more important, it serves to indicate the goal of such a poet as Donne: to reconcile the Many and the One. But if we cannot discard this venerable term, we can at least to some extent displace it by using another term, *meditative poetry,* on all appropriate occasions.

The term *meditative poetry* becomes especially appropriate when we fix our attention upon the total process, the total action, of such poems as Donne's Holy Sonnets, or Divine Meditations, to use the alternative title of some manuscripts. For here is poetry that meets exactly the account that Stevens gives of "modern poetry." It is the poem of the mind, seeking to find what will suffice. It destroys the old romantic tenements, and in their place constructs a stage on which an insatiable actor presents to the mind the action of an inward search. Recall, for example, how frequently Donne places a part of himself as an actor on a stage. It may be the deathbed, as in Holy Sonnet 4, imaged as a scene of legal trial:

> Oh my blacke Soule! now thou art summoned
> By sicknesse, deaths herald, and champion. . .

Or, in an image almost too good to be true for my argument, we have the deathbed stage of Holy Sonnet 6: "This is my playes last scene." It may be "the round earths imagin'd corners" at the Judgment Day (Holy Sonnet 7), or the scene of the Passion (Holy Sonnet 11):

> Spit in my face you Jewes, and pierce my side,
> Buffet, and scoffe, scourge, and crucifie mee,
> For I have sinn'd, and sinn'd, and onely hee,
> Who could do no iniquitie, hath dyed. . .

Or it may be the siege of a city, as in the famous "Batter my heart, three person'd God" (Holy Sonnet 14).

Next, Donne allows this projected part of himself, this actor, to speak, dramatically, its meditated problems on that stage, as in the earlier version of the middle lines of Holy Sonnet 6:

> And gluttonous death, will instantly unjoynt
> My body, and soule, and I shall sleepe a space,
> Or presently, I know not, see that Face,
> Whose feare already shakes my every joynt. . .

Then, in the finale, usually in the whole sestet of the sonnet, this projected self, this insatiable actor, merges with the whole, larger mind of the meditative man, finding what will suffice "In an emotion as of two people, as of two/Emotions becoming one"—to continue with Wallace Stevens' words in "Of Modern Poetry." So, in Holy Sonnet 4, the "blacke Soule" is advised by the larger mind, speaking in a sort of dialogue:

> Yet grace, if thou repent, thou canst not lacke;
> But who shall give thee that grace to beginne?
> Oh make thy selfe with holy mourning blacke,
> And red with blushing, as thou art with sinne;
> Or wash thee in Christs blood, which hath this might
> That being red, it dyes red soules to white.

So, too, at the close of Holy Sonnet 8, we have the dramatic reconciliation of two selves, of actor and mind, or of Soul and Self (to use Yeats's terms), as the total self, the total mind, concludes:

> Then turne
> O pensive soule, to God, for he knows best
> Thy true griefe, for he put it in my breast.

Thy, the actor's, true grief, for he put it in *my*, the whole man's, breast.

Now let us watch the full development of the meditative action in a complete Holy Sonnet, the thirteenth. Here we have what might be called a double stage: an outer stage which is the scene of the Judgment Day, and an inner stage which is the scene of the crucified Christ beheld within the heart of the meditative man:

> What if this present were the worlds last night?
> Mark in my heart, O Soule, where thou dost dwell,
> The picture of Christ crucified, and tell
> Whether that countenance can thee affright. . .

What should the Soul see and ask at such a scene as this? The next quatrain tells us, by blending in its imagery the glory and terror of the Second Coming with the love and mercy of the first:

> Teares in his eyes quench the amasing light,
> Blood fills his frownes, which from his pierc'd head fell.
> And can that tongue adjudge thee unto hell,
> Which pray'd forgiveness for his foes fierce spight?

And now the whole mind of the meditative man begins to explain, answering the projected and implied questions of the Soul:

> No, no; but as in my idolatrie
> I said to all my profane mistresses,
> Beauty, of pitty, foulnesse onely is

A signe of rigour: so I say to thee, [my soul]
To wicked spirits are horrid shapes assign'd,
This beauteous forme assures a pitious minde.

And thus Soul and Self, actor and total mind, are joined in the finding of what will suffice on this occasion. The essential process of all true meditative poetry depends upon the interaction between a projected, dramatized part of the self, and the whole mind of the meditative man.

Such is the interior quest—to find what will suffice—that underlies and directs the course of Donne's entire poetical career. "Seeke wee then our selves in our selves," Donne writes to his friend Rowland Woodward, in one of the verse-letters of his middle years, where Donne looks back upon his own earlier career and regrets that he

to too many'hath showne
How love-song weeds, and Satyrique thornes are growne
Where seeds of better Arts, were early sown.

"Love-song weeds," "Satyrique thornes," "seeds of better Arts" —these are the diverse elements whose peculiar blending constitutes Donne's poetry. Wherever we turn in his poetry, whether early, middle, or late, we are likely to find that his greatest achievements occur when these three elements are struggling toward a reconciliation: the love-song, the satire, and certain "better" arts, among which we must give a primary place to those arts of self-analysis and meditation by which religious men of the late Renaissance sought to find the sufficing poise and stability of religious virtue.

We have already watched the action of this mingling in Holy Sonnet 13, where, using the verse-form along with certain motifs consecrated to Petrarchan ladies, the meditative man speaks scornfully of his idolatry of profane mistresses; but we can see the working of these three elements more clearly if we turn from the poetry of Donne's middle years and watch the materials jostling together in what appear, for the most part, to be among

Donne's earliest poetical efforts, his love-elegies. Here indeed we can find the very rankest growth of love-song weeds in all Donne's poetry (and in fact some of the rankest of the Renaissance), along with a great many harsh satirical thorns. I think those critics are right who have argued that we must regard most of these elegies as witty, primarily literary excursions into the popular libertine mode stemming out of Ovid and reinforced by Montaigne: they show how thoroughly Donne was aware of the libertine aspects of the Renaissance; but they have probably only a slight bearing upon Donne's actual life.

The second Elegy, for instance, is a literary exercise in sheer ingenious fun, as the Roman name of the mistress indicates:

> Marry, and love thy *Flavia*, for shee
> Hath all things, whereby others beautious bee,
> For, though her eyes be small, her mouth is great,
> Though they be Ivory, yet her teeth be jeat,
> Though they be dimme, yet she is light enough,
> And though her harsh haire fall, her skinne is rough. . .
> Though all her parts be not in th'usuall place,
> She'hath yet an Anagram of a good face.

This tone of literary comedy dominates most of the Elegies; and yet I do not mean to dismiss them as insignificant parts of Donne's work. Viewed as a whole, with all their levity, with all their witty, outrageous distortion, the Elegies succeed in creating a powerful sense of the fickleness, the instability, the treachery, of physical existence. Here is a world corrupted by jealousy, spying, deceit, disloyalty, sickness, and death, as in the cruel opening of Elegy 1:

> Fond woman, which would'st have thy husband die,
> And yet complain'st of his great jealousie;
> If swolne with poyson, hee lay in'his last bed,
> His body with a sere-barke covered,
> Drawing his breath, as thick and short, as can
> The nimblest crocheting Musitian,
> Ready with loathsome vomiting to spue

His Soule out of one hell, into a new,
Made deafe with his poore kindreds howling cries,
Begging with few feign'd teares, great legacies,
Thou would'st not weepe, but jolly, 'and frolicke bee,
As a slave, which to morrow should be free;
Yet weep'st thou, when thou seest him hungerly
Swallow his owne death, hearts-bane jealousie.

That is: you want him to die; well, jealousy will kill him, so why complain about his jealousy?

O give him many thanks, he'is courteous,
That in suspecting kindly warneth us.

This sense of decay and disloyalty, we see, is not at all limited to the world of lovers: Donne's images and allusions extend the range of implication to include, first, that glimpse of avaricious kinsmen, and then the outer world of city, kingdom, and church, as in the conclusion of Elegy 1.

Now I see many dangers; for that is
His realme, his castle, and his diocesse.
But if, as envious men, which would revile
Their Prince, or coyne his gold, themselves exile
Into another countrie, 'and doe it there,
Wee play'in another house, what should we feare?
There we will scorne his houshold policies,
His seely plots, and pensionary spies,
As the inhabitants of Thames right side
Do Londons Major [Mayor]; or Germans, the Popes pride.

Thus, too, in Elegy 4 he speaks of the treacherous perfume that has betrayed his presence to a suspicious father:

But Oh, too common ill, I brought with mee
That which betrayed mee to my enemie:
A loud perfume, which at my entrance cryed
Even at thy fathers nose, so were wee spied.
When, like a tyran King, that in his bed
Smelt gunpowder, the pale wretch shivered.

Or in Elegy 11 he speaks thus of the Spanish coins that are corrupting all Europe, those coins

> Which, as the soule quickens head, feet and heart,
> As streames, like veines, run through th'earth's every part,
> Visit all Countries, and have slily made
> Gorgeous *France*, ruin'd, ragged and decay'd;
> *Scotland*, which knew no State, proud in one day:
> And mangled seventeen-headed *Belgia*.

More important, five of the Elegies deal with human insecurity in a much more painful, powerful, and sombre way. Elegy 5, "His Picture," is based upon the speaker's steady consideration of the possibility that his physical handsomeness may be destroyed during a forthcoming military expedition—a clear allusion, it seems, to Donne's participation in the expedition to Cadiz or to the Azores in 1596 or 1597. The lover has given his picture to his lady, and he urges her:

> When weather-beaten I come backe; my hand,
> Perhaps with rude oares torne, or Sun beams tann'd,
> My face and brest of hairecloth, and my head
> With cares rash sodaine stormes, being o'rspread,
> My body'a sack of bones, broken within,
> And powders blew staines scatter'd on my skinne;
> If rivall fooles taxe thee to'have lov'd a man,
> So foule, and course, as, Oh, I may seeme than,
> This shall say what I was: and thou shalt say,
> Doe his hurts reach mee? doth my worth decay?
> Or doe they reach his judging minde, that hee
> Should now love lesse, what hee did love to see?
> That which in him was faire and delicate,
> Was but the milke, which in loves childish state
> Did nurse it: who now is growne strong enough
> To feed on that, which to disused tasts seemes tough.

Miss Helen Gardner[1] has well explained the religious implications of the closing lines, which are built upon traditional dis-

[1] *Modern Language Review*, 39 (1944), 333-7.

tinctions between lower and higher modes of love, with particular reference to the following passage in the Epistle to the Hebrews (5. 12-14):

> ye have need that one teach you again which be the first principles of the oracles of God; and are become such as have need of milk, and not of strong meat. For every one that useth milk is unskilful in the word of righteousness: for he is a babe. But strong meat belongeth to them that are of full age, even those who by reason of use have their senses exercised to discern both good and evil.

The seeds of better arts are indeed beginning to grow beyond the weeds and thorns.

Elegy 12, "His parting from her," shows a lover who is desperately attempting by ingenious vows of constancy to rise above the Ovidian world of flux and mutability, while Elegy 10, "The Dreame," shows another true lover poignantly oppressed by the world's instability:

> So, if I dreame I have you, I have you,
> For all our joyes are but fantasticall.
> And so I scape the paine, for paine is true. . .
> Alas, true joyes at best are *dreame* enough;
> Though you stay here you passe too fast away:
> For even at first lifes *Taper* is a snuffe.

More powerful still, the famous Elegy 16, "By our first strange and fatall interview," gains most of its drama from its view of the various dangers that would beset his mistress if she should accompany him abroad disguised as a page:

> Thy (else Almighty) beautie cannot move
> Rage from the Seas, nor thy love teach them love,
> Nor tame wild Boreas harshnesse; Thou hast reade
> How roughly hee in peeces shivered
> Faire Orithea, whom he swore he lov'd.

And the Elegy concludes with an overwhelming apprehension of physical danger as he begs his mistress:

> nor in bed fright thy Nurse
> With midnights startings, crying out, oh, oh
> Nurse, ô my love is slaine, I saw him goe
> O'r the white Alpes alone; I saw him I,
> Assail'd, fight, taken, stabb'd, bleed, fall, and die.

Consider finally the famous Elegy 9, "The Autumnall" (probably a later composition than most of the other Elegies) —consider how its power lies in this: that the autumnal beauty of this wise, temperate, middle-aged lady is poised so precariously between the gay volatile beauties of youth and the inevitable state of those Donne calls the "*Winter-faces*," "whose skin's slacke;/Lanke, as an unthrifts purse; but a soules sacke." The whole poem is dominated by images of the grave and death, as when he compliments this lady's wrinkles:

> Call not these wrinkles, *graves;* If *graves* they were,
> They were *Loves graves;* for else he is no where.
> Yet lies not Love *dead* here, but here doth sit
> Vow'd to this trench, like an *Anachorit.*
> And here, till hers, which must be his *death,* come,
> He doth not digge a *Grave,* but build a *Tombe.*

Such is the funereal atmosphere which this one rare lady, for the moment, transcends.

In all these ways, then, Donne's love-elegies prepare the way for the shattering portrayal of the world's instability that forms an essential part of the two great *Anniversaries* composed by Donne as he was approaching his fortieth year. At the same time, the Elegies prepare us for the second essential aspect of those *Anniversaries*—the religious counterpoise to the world's decay, an element we have already seen at the close of the fifth Elegy. Sometimes, in the Elegies, these seeds of better arts put forth their sprouts among the weeds and thorns in full awareness of their ironical incongruity—as in the angelic and mystical imagery of the gay Elegy 19, "Going to Bed," or in this passage near the end of Elegy 11, "The Bracelet," a passage which, taken by itself, might almost form a part of some devout prayer:

> But, thou art resolute; Thy will be done!
> Yet with such anguish, as her onely sonne
> The Mother in the hungry grave doth lay,
> Unto the fire these Martyrs I betray.
> Good soules, (for you give life to every thing)
> Good Angels, (for good messages you bring)
> Destin'd you might have beene to such an one,
> As would have lov'd and worship'd you alone:
> One that would suffer hunger, nakednesse,
> Yea death, ere he would make your number lesse.

But of course the Angels here are gold coins, sacrificed according to his mistress's will, in order to replace the lost bracelet. So, among Donne's Elegies, the best are those that, like "The Autumnall," deal primarily with the threat of death and decay; or those other, quite different, Elegies, such as "Going to Bed," where religious images work wittily to effect the disintegration of their native virtue.

But, among Donne's earlier poems, it is in the Satires that we find the most striking example of a successful co-ordination of what I have called the three prime elements of his poetry. Everyone has recognized that, among Donne's five Satires, only the third rises to really distinguished poetry, but exactly why it is successful has not perhaps been adequately estimated. It is, I think, because the poem succeeds in coalescing, absorbing, all the extravagant and wheeling interests that we have seen in the Elegies. Its basic metaphor comes from the love song: the search for the ideal mistress; but the mistress here is true religion:

> Is not our Mistress faire Religion,
> As worthy of all our Soules devotion,
> As vertue was to the first blinded age?

And he proceeds, a few lines later, to play this concept off against the poses of the Elizabethan lover:

and must every hee
Which cryes not, Goddesse, to thy Mistresse, draw,
Or eate thy poysonous words? courage of straw!

Those who love the world, he says, carrying on the image, love only "a withered and worne strumpet," and the problems of the search for true religion are imaged under a series of false mistresses or false attitudes toward woman:

Seeke true religion. O where? Mirreus
Thinking her unhous'd here, and fled from us,
Seekes her at Rome, there, because hee doth know
That shee was there a thousand yeares agoe,
He loves her ragges so, as wee here obey
The statecloth where the Prince sate yesterday.
Crantz to such brave Loves will not be inthrall'd,
But loves her onely, who at Geneva is call'd
Religion, plaine, simple, sullen, yong,
Contemptuous, yet unhansome; As among
Lecherous humors, there is one that judges
No wenches wholsome, but course country drudges.
Graius stayes still at home here, and because
Some Preachers, vile ambitious bauds, and lawes
Still new like fashions, bid him thinke that shee
Which dwels with us, is onely perfect, hee
Imbraceth her, whom his Godfathers will
Tender to him, being tender, as Wards still
Take such wives as their Guardians offer, or
Pay valewes. Carelesse Phrygius doth abhorre
All, because all cannot be good, as one
Knowing some women whores, dares marry none.
Graccus loves all as one, and thinkes that so
As women do in divers countries goe
In divers habits, yet are still one kinde,
So doth, so is Religion. . .

Those Roman names (with the one comic Dutch intrusion), the coarse language, the rough meter, the tone of fierce contempt, all this is part of the poem's satiric base, as the title and the opening have indicated:

> Kinde pitty chokes my spleene, brave scorn forbids
> Those teares to issue which swell my eye-lids;
> I must not laugh, nor weepe sinnes, and be wise,
> Can railing then cure these worne maladies?

And indeed the satiric tone of "railing" dominates the first two-thirds of the poem. Yet it is, curiously, not like the public railing of the Roman satirists. The opening lines suggest a self-address, a self-questioning: a manner which the following lines enforce by coming close to Donne's personal experience: first his sense of apostasy from those "seeds of better Arts":

> and shall thy fathers spirit
> Meete blinde Philosophers in heaven, whose merit
> Of strict life may be imputed faith, and heare
> Thee, whom hee taught so easie wayes and neare
> To follow, damn'd?

And then that Donne who was willing to sail off on the military expeditions to Cadiz and the Azores:

> Dar'st thou ayd mutinous Dutch, and dar'st thou lay
> Thee in ships woodden Sepulchres, a prey
> To leaders rage, to stormes, to shot, to dearth?

So the exhortations continue, from beginning to end:

> Foole and wretch, wilt thou let thy Soule be tyed
> To mans lawes, by which she shall not be tryed
> At the last day?

Are these the public exhortations of the satirist, or the intimate self-addresses of one who knows how to practice the religious art of seeking himself in himself? They are both, simultaneously; in this hovering between the public and the meditative voice lies the essential art of the poem. It belongs to no single genre: it is neither purely satiric nor purely meditative; it is a unique and perfectly Donneian blending of love-song weeds, satiric thorns, and those better arts sown early in his life.

Lastly, we must note the curious compounding of these elements that occurs frequently among Donne's "Songs and Sonets." Consider, for example, "Twicknam garden." This is a poem that has puzzled students of Donne, since the title alludes to the Countess of Bedford's estate, which she occupied in 1608: this is a fairly late poem, then; and Donne is a thoroughly married man. Can it be that Donne has developed feelings about the Countess of Bedford as strong as those developed in the poem? There is more than courtly compliment of a patron here. What does it all mean?

Perhaps the poem has nothing at all to do with the Countess of Bedford in person, but only with her garden, which the lover has used as an imagistic contrast with his own state of mind, as a stage upon which he can seek himself in himself, by projecting there his tormented sense of grief:

> Blasted with sighs, and surrounded with teares,
> Hither I come to seeke the spring,
> And at mine eyes, and at mine eares,
> Receive such balmes, as else cure every thing;
> But O, selfe traytor, I do bring
> The spider love, which transubstantiates all,
> And can convert Manna to gall,
> And that this place may thoroughly be thought
> True Paradise, I have the serpent brought.

This actor is a traitor to himself: love in his case is a poisonous spider, which transubstantiates, in a bitter way, all life-giving elements. He has brought the serpent within himself to this place. Why? Because, the next stanza tells us, he is in love, and yet in some "disgrace" at the same time: *disgrace*, a rich word, which in this context seems to carry the full range of its many implications: a state of disfavor, dishonor, reproach, and humiliation:

> But that I may not this disgrace
> Indure, nor yet leave loving, Love let mee
> Some senslesse peece of this place bee;
> Make me a mandrake, so I may groane here,
> Or a stone fountaine weeping out my yeare.

He feels called upon to protest his fidelity through a strained and curious conceit that suggests a Petrarchan service of communion:

> Hither with christall vyals, lovers come,
>   And take my teares, which are loves wine,
>   And try your mistresse Teares at home,
> For all are false, that tast not just like mine;
>   Alas, hearts do not in eyes shine,
> Nor can you more judge womans thoughts by teares,
>   Then by her shadow, what she weares.
> O perverse sexe, where none is true but shee,
>   Who's therefore true, because her truth kills mee.

What shall we make of this satirical outburst, especially the last two lines? On the surface they seem to carry a conventional meaning: that some true woman has denied this lover her favor, for she is true to someone else, or to some principle. Yet there may also be the deeper suggestion that this lover's grief comes from the fact that he has in some way trespassed, or is accused of having trespassed, against the loyalty and love of the one woman whom he truly loves and who truly loves him. Perhaps the sighs and tears of the opening line are hers as well as his, the sighs and tears of a woman whose "truth" fills this suspected and perhaps erring lover with a killing sense of grief.

Similarly, we may gain a deeper appreciation of Donne's great "Nocturnall upon S. Lucies day, Being the shortest day," if we disregard the coincidence that the Countess of Bedford's name happened to be Lucy. It seems probable that the poem is related to the death of Donne's wife in August 1617, the loss which Donne commemorated in the seventeenth Holy Sonnet. If this is so, the "Nocturnall" was written more than two years after Donne had become a priest of the English church. There is nothing incongruous here, for the poem holds strong religious implications: its title suggests the "nocturn," a division of the office of Matins traditionally performed at midnight, while the

"Vigill" of the conclusion evokes the same atmosphere of religious devotion. This poem, like the early Satire 3, displays Donne's representative texture, a blending of the love-song, the satire, and the meditation, but here, as would befit a priest, the meditative form is dominant. One need not recall that Donne's rash and ruinous marriage had occurred in December[2] to read this poem as another of his "anniversaries," set in the symbolical darkness of the year's longest night, the eve of December 13 in the old calendar.

We may take the poem, then, as one of the final achievements in Donne's lifelong effort to control his sense of the dissolution and fragility of worldly things: for with the death of this most loved of bodily things Donne's sense of the world's emptiness has reached an absolute conclusion. Isaak Walton, in his Life of Donne, has given us an appropriate setting for this poem, when he speaks of how Donne buried "with his tears, all his earthly joys in his most dear and deserving wives grave; and betook himself to a most retired and solitary life." "In this retiredness," Walton continues, "he became *crucified to the world*, and all those vanities, those imaginary pleasures that are daily acted on that restless stage . . . for now his very soul was elemented of nothing but sadness; now, grief took so full a possession of his heart, as to leave no place for joy." [3]

So it is with the "Nocturnall," where the first stanza builds a sombre stage upon which this speaker may project his own sense of deadness:

> Tis the yeares midnight, and it is the dayes,
> Lucies, who scarce seaven houres herself unmaskes,
> The Sunne is spent, and now his flasks
> Send forth light squibs, no constant rayes;
> The worlds whole sap is sunke:

[2] Donne says in a letter: "about three weeks before Christmas [1601] we married." See Edmund Gosse, *The Life and Letters of John Donne* (2 vols., London, 1899), I, 101.

[3] Isaak Walton, *Lives*, World's Classics (London, 1927), p. 51.

The generall balme th'hydroptique earth hath drunk,
Whither, as to the beds feet, life is shrunke,
Dead and enterr'd; yet all these seeme to laugh,
Compar'd with mee, who am their Epitaph.

Having projected this aspect of himself, he proceeds, in a meditative way, to analyse that state of mind:

Study me then, you who shall lovers bee
At the next world, that is, at the next Spring:
For I am every dead thing,
In whom love wrought new Alchimie.
For his art did expresse
A quintessence even from nothingnesse,
From dull privations, and leane emptinesse:
He ruin'd mee, and I am re-begot
Of absence, darknesse, death; things which are not.

"Oft a flood/Have wee two wept, and so/Drownd the whole world, us two," he recalls, alluding perhaps to the kind of situation dramatized in his "Valediction: of weeping"; "oft did we grow/To be two Chaosses, when we did show/Care to ought else," he continues, alluding perhaps to the kind of situation dramatized in "Twicknam garden"; "and often absences /Withdrew our soules, and made us carcasses," he adds, alluding perhaps to the kind of situation dramatized in his "Valediction: forbidding mourning."

But I am by her death, (which word wrongs her)
Of the first nothing, the Elixer grown;
Were I a man, that I were one,
I needs must know; I should preferre,
If I were any beast,
Some ends, some means; Yea plants, yea stones detest,
And love; All, all some properties invest;
If I an ordinary nothing were,
As shadow, a light, and body must be here.

"But I am None"; he declares, "nor will my Sunne [the beloved] renew."

Then, in a vehement resolution, he turns upon all worldly lovers with one harsh satirical thorn that demolishes all their love-song weeds; and he ends by preparing himself to join his beloved in the after-life, thus converting the conventional "Saint" of Petrarchan poetry—the saint of rose and ice—into the image of a true religious goal:

> You lovers, for whose sake, the lesser Sunne
> At this time to the Goat is runne
> To fetch new lust, and give it you,
> Enjoy your summer all;
> Since shee enjoyes her long nights festivall,
> Let mee prepare towards her, and let mee call
> This hour her Vigill, and her Eve, since this
> Both the years, and the dayes deep midnight is.

So, in Wallace Stevens' terms, the meditative poet has given us the poem of the mind, in the act of finding what will suffice. He has built a sombre stage; he has placed an aspect of himself as "Epitaph" upon that stage; and he has allowed that insatiable actor, slowly and with meditation, to speak like a metaphysician in the dark.

II

John Donne:
A Valediction

IT HAS now been more than forty years since that memorable date, October 20, 1921, when T. S. Eliot publicly observed that Donne and his fellow poets could "feel their thought as immediately as the odour of a rose." [1] It is a date worthy of some ceremony, since no critical remark of our century has had a more profound effect upon the study of English poetry. Eliot's essay "The Metaphysical Poets" came as a focusing of blurred and flickering insights that had been developing throughout the late Victorian and the Edwardian eras: Arthur Symons as far back as 1899 had found in Donne's poetry a "rapture in which the mind is supreme, a reasonable rapture." "This lover loves with his whole nature, and so collectedly because reason, in him, is not in conflict with passion, but passion's ally." [2] Issuing as the culmination of this long-developing view, Eliot's twin theories of the "unification of sensibility" and its subsequent "dissociation"

[1] T. S. Eliot, "The Metaphysical Poets," *Selected Essays* (New York, Harcourt, Brace & Co., 1932), p. 247; originally published as a leading article in *The Times Literary Supplement*.

[2] See Joseph E. Duncan, "The Revival of Metaphysical Poetry, 1872-1912," *PMLA*, 68 (1953), 658-71; now incorporated in Mr. Duncan's book, *The Revival of Metaphysical Poetry: The History of a Style, 1800 to the Present* (Minneapolis, University of Minnesota Press, 1959). See Arthur Symons' essay on Donne in *Fortnightly Review*, n.s. 66 (1899), 741.

were bound to have "a success in the world astonishing to their author," as Eliot observed in 1947, when he permitted us to read John Milton once again.[3] But these theories about the "fusion of thought and feeling" have now clearly run their course. Within the past few years Mr. Kermode has argued that the whole hypothesis was only a fallacious effort to find historical justification for the Symbolist aesthetic of the Image; Mr. Unger has argued that "there was no unique fusion" in Donne's poetry, no evidence of "unified sensibility," but only "an urgent search for unity"; and Mr. Hunt, who deeply admires Donne, nevertheless has told us that for true unification we ought to look toward Spenser and Milton, for Donne was a poet of extraordinary limitations: "an ear relatively dull to the sonorities of language; a limited sensory response and an insensitivity to many subtleties of emotion; a lack of pleasure in the beauties of the natural world and an inability to invest its physical facts with the aura of the romantic imagination; an absence of any strong feeling for the cultural traditions of his own civilization, or of any strong sense of personal community with the rest of mankind; and a certain deficiency in human sympathy." [4]

Perhaps it is time, then, to pronounce a valediction, in Donne's own kind, admitting mutability in the world, but affirming the immortality of certain true relationships—in particular, the deep and valid relation between Donne and the later age that loved him: an age that might have applied to Donne's poetry these lines from Donne's own "Valediction: of the book":

> When this booke is made thus,
> Should againe the ravenous

[3] T. S. Eliot, "Milton II," *On Poetry and Poets* (London, Faber & Faber, 1957), p. 152.

[4] Frank Kermode, *Romantic Image* (London, Routledge & Kegan Paul, 1957), Chap. 8. Leonard Unger, "Fusion and Experience," *The Man in the Name* (Minneapolis, University of Minnesota Press, 1956), p. 123. Clay Hunt, *Donne's Poetry* (New Haven, Yale University Press, 1954), p. 148.

Vandals and Goths inundate us,
Learning were safe; in this our Universe
Schooles might learne Science, Spheares Musick, Angels Verse.

The timing of Eliot's famous essay indicates the basis of this liaison. The essay came, in 1921, just as William Butler Yeats was deep within the composition of his private guide to "Unity of Being," *A Vision*, which appeared in 1925. In composing the *Vision*, Yeats tells us, he learned from his mysterious teachers that he must, in effect, feel his thought, or, in his own words, "give concrete expression to their abstract thought." ". . . And if my mind returned too soon to their unmixed abstraction they [his 'communicators'] would say, 'We are starved.' " [5] The essay came, too, as I. A. Richards was conceiving his *Principles of Literary Criticism*, which appeared in 1924, offering us the poetry of "inclusion," as represented in Donne's "Nocturnall upon S. Lucies day"; such poetry, for Richards, offered a way by which modern man might achieve the "resolution of a welter of disconnected impulses into a single ordered response"—with the resultant consciousness of "completed being" that for Richards comes from participation in the greatest art.[6]

That Donne seemed to answer this general quest for unity of being is made especially plain by Eliot in a note on Donne that he wrote for *The Nation and the Athenaeum* in 1923, by way of "inquiry into the reasons for Donne's present popularity." Casting aside all matters of mere fashion, all accidental relationships, he asserts the one basic cause: Donne's "mind has unity and order." "The range of his feeling was great, but no more remarkable than its unity. He was altogether present in every thought and in every feeling." Our age, he says, "objects to the simplification and separation of the mental faculties." "Ethics having been eclipsed by psychology, we accept the belief that

[5] W. B. Yeats, *A Vision* (New York, Macmillan Co., 1938), p. 12.
[6] I. A. Richards, *Principles of Literary Criticism* (New York, Harcourt, Brace & Co., 1948), Chap. 32.

any state of mind is extremely complex, and chiefly composed of odds and ends in constant flux manipulated by desire and fear. When, therefore, we find a poet who neither suppresses nor falsifies, and who expresses complicated states of mind, we give him welcome." [7] The last sentence might almost have been written by Richards.

What Eliot, and Richards, and Yeats all admired in Donne has been brilliantly summed up by Wallace Stevens when he wrote that modern poetry must give "The poem of the mind in the act of finding/What will suffice." We must emphasize the *act of finding.* For Donne presents the very process by which unity of mind is discovered: he does indeed, as Mr. Unger says, present the search for unity, in all the agony of its exploration, but in the end of every great poem that he wrote, his speaker has discovered "what will suffice":

> If our two loves be one, or, thou and I
> Love so alike, that none doe slacken, none can die.
>
> But wee will have a way more liberall,
> Then changing hearts, to joyne them, so wee shall
> Be one, and one anothers All.
>
> Let us love nobly, and live, and adde againe
> Yeares and yeares unto yeares, till we attaine
> To write threescore: this is the second of our raigne.
>
> But wonder at a greater wonder, for to us
> Created nature doth these things subdue,
> But their Creator, whom sin, nor nature tyed,
> For us, his Creatures, and his foes, hath dyed.
>
> And, having done that, Thou hast done,
> I feare no more.

[7] T. S. Eliot, "John Donne," *The Nation and the Athenaeum,* 33 (1923), 331-2.

After so many decades of talk about Donne's "anguish of the marrow" and the contraries that met to vex him, it is perhaps too easy to forget the noble serenity of these conclusions; yet the movement from anguish and vexation to the finding of what will suffice is the essential action of Donne's poetry and of his entire life. Whether it is the early Satire 3, or the late "Anniversaries," or the even later (I think) "Nocturnall upon S. Lucies day," the essential action of the mind is the same. The typical Donneian poem opens with a vision of the follies and foibles and infidelities of the world, sometimes given in a comic tone, as in "The Sunne Rising," where that "pedantique wretch," the sun, insists on arising punctually, only to reveal the sorry world of time-servers:

> goe chide
> Late schoole boyes, and sowre prentices,
> Goe tell Court-huntsmen, that the King will ride,
> Call countrey ants to harvest offices;
> Love, all alike, no season knowes, nor clyme,
> Nor houres, dayes, moneths, which are the rags of time.

Or it may be the fierce and bitter opening of a holy sonnet:

> If poysonous mineralls, and if that tree,
> Whose fruit threw death on else immortall us,
> If lecherous goats, if serpents envious
> Cannot be damn'd; Alas; why should I bee?

Or it may be the sombre vision of universal decay in the "Nocturnall":

> The Sunne is spent, and now his flasks
> Send forth light squibs, no constant rayes;
> The worlds whole sap is sunke:
> The generall balme th' hydroptique earth hath drunk . . .

But whatever the mood and tone, whatever the vision of time and decay, whatever the era of Donne's life, "the poem of the act of the mind," as Stevens would call it, moves steadily onward to the finding of what will suffice. Sometimes it is found in carnal love:

> This bed thy center is, these walls, thy spheare.

Sometimes in the operation of Grace:

> That thou remember them, some claime as debt,
> I thinke it mercy, if thou wilt forget.

Sometimes in death and the after-life:

> Since shee enjoys her long nights festivall,
> Let mee prepare towards her, and let mee call
> This houre her Vigill, and her Eve, since this
> Both the yeares, and the dayes deep midnight is.

Why should we find, nowadays, a tendency to deny unity to the mind that could execute so perfect a movement? For two reasons, I believe. First, because Eliot's theory of unification and dissociation was grossly unfair to Milton and other poets: in an effort to defend Milton or Shelley, critics have been led to counterattack. More important, however, is a serious fallacy in the assumption that underlies most criticism based on the doctrine of the unified sensibility. The assumption is implicit in Eliot's phrase "mechanism of sensibility"; in Williamson's view that the fusion of learning and passion in Donne was "spontaneous and natural"; in Ransom's early contention that the term "metaphysical" ought to be equated with "miraculous," since the unity in metaphysical poetry was achieved by a "miracle" of metaphor.[8] All these views assume that Donne's alleged power of unification was something given, native, inherent in the fortunate man and the more fortunate age; something inexplicable and magical that Donne and his age possessed, and we do not.

[8] Eliot, *Selected Essays*, p. 247. George Williamson, *The Donne Tradition* (Cambridge, Harvard University Press, 1930), p. 48. John Crowe Ransom, *The World's Body* (New York, Charles Scribner's Sons, 1938), pp. 133-42.

This attitude is not very far from Matthew Arnold's weary cry in "The Scholar Gipsy": "O Life unlike to ours!" "Thou hadst *one* aim, *one* business, *one* desire"—"And we imagine thee exempt from age . . . Because thou hadst—what we, alas, have not!"

But such a view will not describe the action of Donne's poetry. The unity enacted within his poetry was not a gift: it was a unity achieved in much the same way that Eliot and Yeats and Hopkins and Paul Claudel were later to follow—the way of arduous and disciplined meditation. It is ironical that Eliot, around 1930, should have lost his early confidence in Donne, just as he himself was beginning to follow a mode of inner life that Donne had known from his childhood; yet Eliot almost predicted this result in his note of 1923, when he concluded: "We cannot have any order but our own, but from Donne and his contemporaries we can draw instruction and encouragement." Encouragement, we might say, came from Donne and his fellow poets; instruction, toward a unified meditative action, came in part from a Spanish contemporary of Donne's who died in 1591: St. John of the Cross. Eliot's debt to the spiritual writings of St. John of the Cross has been widely recognized by the commentators on *Ash Wednesday, Murder in the Cathedral,* and the *Quartets;* the debt extends even to the essential organization and inner process of the *Quartets,* which enact a spiritual progress from meditation to contemplation, after the manner prescribed by St. John of the Cross in his subtle treatises of self-analysis.

If this is so, then the total careers of Donne and Eliot bear the most profound analogy; both, we may say, spent their lives in an arduous effort to achieve the state of mind described by Paul Claudel in his prose meditation, *A Poet before the Cross,* where Claudel envisions a state of mind which is "both infinitely multiple and intensely one." "From the north to the south, from alpha to omega, from the east to the west, all is one with us, we are clothed with it, we instigate it, we are both revealed and humbled in this orchestral operation. . . . Our brief blind impulses are wedded, revived, interpreted and developed in immense stellar movements. Outside of us, at astronomical distances, we decipher the text microscopically inscribed in the bottom of our hearts." "With all our senses we shall contemplate the first cause." We shall work "with an intelligence so clear and informed that it will become as immediate as sensation is in us, with a fidelity of all our being, with a will as prompt and subtle as the flame of a fire."[9] Those words of Claudel, written between 1933 and 1935, at the height of the vogue for Donne, describe the central action of all meditative poetry, the central action of Donne, Herbert, Crashaw, Vaughan, and Marvell, the central action of Hopkins, Dickinson, Yeats, Eliot, and Claudel.[10]

If I seem to be exaggerating the importance of the act of meditation for the poetry of Donne, we may turn to Donne's own testimony in a verse letter to Rowland Woodward, written, it seems, while Donne was in his early thirties. It is a poem that displays the typical Donneian movement. It opens with the usual satire against the infidelities of the world (including his own):

> Like one who'in her third widdowhood doth professe
> Her selfe a Nunne, tyed to retirednesse,
> So'affects my muse now, a chast fallownesse;
>
> Since shee to few, yet to too many'hath showne
> How love-song weeds, and Satyrique thornes are growne
> Where seeds of better Arts, were early sown.

[9] Paul Claudel, *A Poet before the Cross*, trans. Wallace Fowlie (Chicago, Henry Regnery Co., 1958), pp. 92-3, 150-51.

[10] And of the "greater Romantic lyric" as well: see the admirable essay by M. H. Abrams, "Structure and Style in the Greater Romantic Lyric," in *From Sensibility to Romanticism: Essays Presented to Frederick A. Pottle*, ed. Frederick W. Hilles and Harold Bloom (New York, Oxford University Press, 1965), pp. 527-60: here Abrams shows how certain Romantic poems, particularly by Coleridge and Wordsworth, exemplify a distinctively Romantic mode of meditation, analogous to the meditative action found in certain seventeenth-century poems.

Where seeds of better Arts, were early sown. What were these better Arts that came before the love-songs and the satires? The rest of the poem seems to tell us, at least in part. They include the arts by which, "If our Soules have stain'd their first white, yet wee/May cloth them with faith, and deare honestie." And the method?

> Seeke wee then our selves in our selves; for as
> Men force the Sunne with much more force to passe,
> By gathering his beames with a christall glasse;
>
> So wee, If wee into our selves will turne,
> Blowing our sparkes of vertue, may outburne
> The straw, which doth about our hearts sojourne. . . .
>
> Wee are but farmers of our selves, yet may,
> If we can stocke our selves, and thrive, uplay
> Much, much deare treasure for the great rent day.

It seems fair to say, then, that John Donne's literary career, like that of Eliot or Yeats or Claudel or Hopkins, represents a record of the farming of the self, the stocking of the self, the gathering of the beams of the self into one intense and burning focus. And if such ways of meditation, as Donne seems to say, were learned by Donne *before* the writing of his love-song weeds and satiric thorns, it will not be illegitimate to expect some impact of this meditative discipline upon the writing of those songs and satires. This is not to argue that the "Songs and Sonets" are really religious meditations in rake's clothing; though I believe that the "Nocturnall" is a deeply religious poem. But for most of Donne's love-poetry and satires, one should say no more than this: that it is the inward farming of the self which gives these poems their distinctive structure, direction, and inclusiveness.

It is upon this inward base that most of Donne's poems organize themselves: the strong satirical texture that runs throughout his poetry forms an essential part of the inward quest. The universe cannot be reorganized about an inward center unless the outward straw "which doth about our hearts sojourne" is first burned away. The "naked thinking heart" will not reveal itself without this burning. One is reminded of Eliot's strong satirical vein, and of Claudel, who in the midst of a meditation on the words, "My God, My God, why hast thou forsaken me?" is able to give us the following satirical disquisition:

> What? What is he saying? . . . *Eli* . . . *Eli*. . . . Did you hear what he just said? No, but did you hear it? Allow me, gentlemen and dear colleagues, to call your attention to the decisive confession which the inexorable torture of scientific investigation has just snatched from ignorance and superstition and imposture. . . . I am sure that the root *El* we find on Sumerian inscriptions and Arabic tombs will intrigue the old campaigners of Semitic philology. Whether you see in it a Mesopotamian totem, or a Hittite allusion, or a Moon lover, it is undeniable in any case that in this syllable which has so curiously reached our ears you find the origin of that *Elohim* which in opposition to *Jahveh*, has generously stained in blue the pages of our polychrome Bible. . . . I consider the form *Sabachthani* doubtful and even shocking, and I am almost ready to agree with delightful Professor Pumpernickel who finds in it a Galilean deformation. *Eli, Eli,* or *Eloi* (another form of the vocative) *why have you abandoned me?* Why did he abandon our attractive subject? I see, gentlemen and dear colleagues, and you, ladies who grace this meeting, by the smiles on your faces, I see that no one of you would be embarrassed to answer this naïve question. (*op. cit.*, pp. 124-5)

The colloquialism, the range of the learning, the bitter ironies are akin to Donne; and if this tirade furthermore reminds us of the speeches of Eliot's Knights in *Murder in the Cathedral*, the reminiscence may be more than coincidental. Such racy outbursts are likely to play an important part in any meditative vision of the world.

So then, one might use the word "meditative," rather than "metaphysical," in discussing these poets, for "meditative" seems to point directly toward the inner organizing principle of this poetry, and thus to provide a term of greater discrimination. It might be said, for example, that Ransom and Tate, or Auden and MacNeice, are modern metaphysicals, just as Sam Johnson could find "the metaphysick style" in Donne, Ben Jonson, Suckling, Waller, Denham, Cowley, or Cleveland. But of all these poets only Donne and Tate could truly be called *meditative* poets. The term "meditative," as I see it, does not serve to replace the term "metaphysical"; it rather intersects the term "metaphysical," and serves a different purpose by associating Donne with a powerful tradition in European religious life. Reading Donne in the context of European meditative literature may help us to see more clearly the nature of his greatness, and to grasp his firm centrality in the life of his age and our own.

But can we ever give a satisfying and precise definition of meditative poetry? We might begin by saying that meditative poetry displays an actor who, first of all, seeks himself in himself; but not because he is self-centered in our sense of that term— no, he seeks himself in himself in order to discover or to construct a firm position from which he can include the universe. If we go on to look for a more detailed account of this meditative action, we may find it suggested in the following words of Paul Claudel:

> Thus we understand that the soul is not . . . a kind of fluid fabricated somehow or other which the body yields like a gas-generator. On the contrary, everything takes place as if there were a motor-directive principle governing our organized matter, and as if there were in us someone who is master and who knows what he has to do with everything. It is not our body which makes us, it is we at each second who make our body and who compose it in that attitude adapted to every situation which we call sensation and perception. It is not movement which drags us along in an irresistible flow. Movement is at our disposal. We can exploit it. We who are able to oppose and stop it, and, by using a free and limit-

less choice, impose on our perceptions the firm pattern of a concept, of a figure, of a will. (*op. cit.*, pp. 196-7)

It is, at least, exactly what the last generation found remarkable in Donne: that he could impose on his perceptions "the firm pattern of a concept, of a figure, of a will."

III

Meditative Action and "The Metaphysick Style"

MEDITATIVE poetry is found in various periods of the world's history: it appears frequently in the Psalms, and some of my students from Asia have told me that it may be found in the poetry of China, Persia, and India. But my purpose here is to examine the nature of the meditative action in English poetry of the seventeenth century and to explore, in relation to this action, the meaning that may still be found in Samuel Johnson's faithful account of "the metaphysick style."

The nature of meditative poetry in seventeenth-century England may be defined by studying its close relation to the practice of religious meditation in that era. The relationship is shown by the poem's own internal action, as the mind engages in acts of interior dramatization. The speaker accuses himself; he talks to God within the self; he approaches the love of God through memory, understanding, and will; he sees, hears, smells, tastes, touches by imagination the scenes of Christ's life as they are represented on a mental stage. Essentially, the meditative action consists of an interior drama, in which a man projects a self upon an inner stage, and there comes to know that self in the light of a divine presence.

To understand the "art of meditation" as it was taught and practiced in Donne's time, one may turn to a neat and compact treatise entitled "The Practical Methode of Meditation," written by the underground Jesuit Edward Dawson for an English audience, and published on the Continent in 1614.[1] Dawson's treatise, written at the peak of the period's intense concern with the "method" of meditation, sums up the principles that had gradually come to dominate the meditative life of the Continent, primarily through the influence of the *Spiritual Exercises* of Ignatius Loyola. Dawson's handbook is in fact a paraphrase of the *Spiritual Exercises*, with adaptations and extensions prompted, as he says, by "approved Authors and experience." He gives the essence of the advice for meditation that was being offered by spiritual counselors throughout Europe, as well as by the numerous underground priests in England. At the same time this advice was being offered in dozens of popular treatises on meditation that were circulating in thousands of copies throughout Europe, and in England as well.

Dawson shows by his blunt, simple, "practical" manner the way in which the art of meditation might become part of the everyday life of everyman. The matter-of-fact tone of the treatise, indeed, helps to convey its central and pervasive assumptions: that man, whether he will or not, lives in the intimate presence of God, and that his first duty in life is to cultivate an awareness of that presence. Thus arises the whole elaborate ceremony of meditation: the careful preparation of materials the night before; the "practice of the presence of God," as it was called, before actual meditation; the preparatory prayers; the preludes; the deliberate, orderly operation of the "three powers of the soul"—memory, understanding, will; and the conclusion in "some affectionate speach" or colloquy with God or the saints, in which "wee may talke with God as a servant with his Maister, as a sonne with his Father, as one friend with another,

[1] Reprinted in *The Meditative Poem*, ed. L. L. Martz (New York, Anchor Books and New York University Press, 1963), pp. 3-23. Unless otherwise noted, all the subsequent quotations concerning the practice of meditation are taken from this treatise.

as a spouse with her beloved bridgrome, or as a guilty prisoner with his Judge, or in any other manner which the holy Ghost shall teach us." The aim of meditation is to apprehend the reality and the meaning of the presence of God with every faculty at man's command. The body must first learn its proper behavior during the ceremony: hence we have detailed advice on whether to kneel, or walk, or sit, or stand. The five senses must learn how to bend their best efforts toward this end: hence the elaborately detailed explanation of the Jesuit "application of the senses" to the art of meditation. Everyday life must come to play its part, for the meditative man must feel that the presence of God is here, now, on his own hearth, in his own stable, and in the deep center of the mind: thus "we may help our selves much to the framing of spirituall conceites [thoughts], if we apply unto our matter familiar similitudes, drawne from our ordinary actions, and this as well in historicall, as spirituall meditations." That is to say, analogies from the world of daily actions must be brought to bear upon the history of the life of Christ, as well as upon such matters as the problem of sin and the excellence of the virtues.

Among all the varied ways of using the senses and physical life in meditation, the most important, most effective, and most famous is the prelude known as the "composition of place." This brilliant Ignatian invention, to which the Jesuit *Exercises* owe a large part of their power, is given its full and proper emphasis by Dawson: "for on the well making of this *Preludium* depends both the understanding of the mystery, and attention in our meditation." Whatever the subject may be, the imagination, the image-making power of man, must endeavor to represent it "so lively, as though we saw [it] indeed, with our corporall eyes." For historical matters, such as events in the life of Christ or a saint, we must visualize the scene in the most vivid and exact detail, "by imagining our selves to be really present at those places." In treating spiritual subjects we must gain the same end by creating "some similitude, answerable to the matter." Thus, for the Last Things, Death, Judgment, Hell, and Heaven, the similitude may be created by imagining the scene in detail, by creating, for example, a likeness of one's self on the deathbed, "forsaken of the Physitians, compassed about with our weeping friends, and expecting our last agony." But the similitude may also be much more figurative: the word "similitude," in seventeenth-century usage, could refer to any kind of parable, allegory, simile, or metaphor. Dawson, discussing the preparation for meditation, suggests that we should "begin to take some tast of our meditation" before the actual performance begins, by stirring up the "affections," the emotions, appropriate to each meditation: "Which we may performe more easily," he adds, "yf we keep in our mind some similitude answering to the affection we would have." And later he suggests that, among several dramatic ways of strengthening these affections, we may sometimes proceed by "faygning [imagining] the very vertues in some venerable shape bewayling their neglect." Thus too he notes that, in the opening similitude for the meditation on sins, "we may imagine our soule to be cast out of Paradise, and to be held prisoner in this body of ours, fettered with the chaines of disordinate Passions, and affections, and clogged with the burden of our owne flesh." In short, this insistence upon "seeing the place" and upon the frequent use of "similitudes" in meditation invites every man to use his image-making faculty with the utmost vigor, in order to ensure a concrete, dramatic setting within which the meditative action may develop. Upon the inward stage of that scene or similitude, the memory, the understanding, and the will may then proceed to explore and understand and feel the proper role of the self in relation to the divine omnipotence and charity. Thus heaven and earth are brought together in the mind; and human action is placed in a responsive, intimate relation with the supernatural.

Only one important qualification needs to be added to the

advice of Dawson. In the Ignatian way, he insists that every meditation must begin with some vivid "composition," but we should not be led to expect that every meditative poem will begin with some vivid scene or symbol. Many do so, directly or implicitly, with the speaker present, for example, at some scene in the life of Christ; but many meditative poems also begin simply with a brief, terse statement of the problem or theme to be explored:

> Why are wee by all creatures waited on?
>
> Why do I languish thus, drooping and dull . . .
>
> Come, come, what doe I here?
>
> I Sing the *Name* which none can say,
> But touch't with an interiour *Ray*,
> The *Name* of our *New Peace*, our *Good*,
> Our *Blisse*, and supernaturall *Blood*,
> The *Name* of all our Lives, and Loves.
>
> What Love is this of thine, that Cannot bee
>   In thine Infinity, O Lord, Confinde,
> Unless it in thy very Person see,
>   Infinity, and Finity Conjoyn'd?

Such openings, though not mentioned by Dawson, are advised by other writers for abstract topics, particularly by St. François de Sales, who notes, "It is true that we may use some similitude or comparison to assist us in the consideration of these subjects," but he fears that the making of "such devices" may prove burdensome, and thus for the meditation of "invisible things" he advises one to begin with "a simple proposal" of the theme.[2] A meditative poem, then, will tend to open in any one of three

[2] See St. Francis de Sales, *Introduction to the Devout Life* (1609), tr. and ed. by John K. Ryan (New York, Image Books, 1955), pp. 83-4. The whole treatise, especially the second part, is of the utmost interest to anyone concerned with studying the details of meditative practice in this era.

ways: (1) with a vivid participation in some scene in the life of Christ or a saint; (2) with a "similitude, answerable to the matter," that is, with some imaginary setting or metaphorical representation; (3) with a "simple proposal" of the issue to be considered.

With the event or theme thus firmly presented within a "recollected" mind fully aware of the presence of God, the meditative action of the three powers of the soul begins to develop each "point" (usually three) into which the long process of meditation (usually lasting an hour) has been divided during the period of preparation. It is evident from Dawson's account that the operation of the memory is inseparable from and continuous with the opening composition or proposal; for the role of memory is to set forth the subject with all its necessary "persons, wordes, and workes." The understanding then proceeds to analyze ("discourse" upon) the meaning of the topic, in relation to the individual self, until gradually the will takes fire and the appropriate personal affections arise. It is clear too from Dawson's account that these affections of the will inevitably lead into the colloquy, where the speaker utters his fears and hopes, his sorrows and joys, in "affectionate speach" before God. The full process of meditation always ends with such a colloquy, but, as Dawson points out, "We may make such manner of speaches in other places of our meditation, and it will be best, and almost needfull so to do."

At the same time, the interior drama will tend to have a firm construction, for the process of meditation, in treating each "point," will tend to display a threefold movement, according with the action of that interior trinity, memory, understanding, and will. Now and then we may find this threefold process echoed or epitomized within the borders of a short poem; or we may find the process suggested at length in a long poem such as Southwell's "Saint Peters Complaint" or Crashaw's "On the name of Jesus"; or we may find it suggested by a sequence of short poems, as in the poems of Traherne in the Dobell manuscript.[3] But what one should expect to find, more often, is some part of the whole meditative action, set down as particularly memorable, perhaps in accordance with the kind of self-examination advised by Dawson under the heading: "What is to be done after Meditation." One is urged here to scrutinize carefully the manner in which one has performed every part of the meditative process, from preparation through colloquy; to examine closely the distractions, consolations, or desolations that one may have experienced; and finally, to "note in some little booke those thinges which have passed in our Meditation, or some part of them, if we think them worth the paynes." Meditative poems present such memorable moments of self-knowledge, affections of sorrow and love, colloquies with the divine presence, recollected and preserved through the aid of the kindred art of poetry.

Meditation points toward poetry in its use of images, in its technique of arousing the passionate affections of the will, in its suggestion that the ultimate reach of meditation is found in the advice of Paul to the Ephesians: "Be filled with the Spirit; speaking to yourselves in psalms and hymns and spiritual songs, singing and making melody in your heart to the Lord." A meditative poem, then, represents the convergence of two arts upon a single object: in English poetry of the late Renaissance the art of meditation entered into and transformed its kindred art of poetry. To express its highest reaches, the art of meditation drew upon all the poetical resources available in the culture of its day. Southwell, writing in an era dominated by the uninspired verse of the poetical miscellanies—with their heavy-footed, alliterative style and their doggerel ballad-stanzas—could use his meditative techniques, along with his knowledge of Italian poetry, to impart a new and startling vigor even to a moribund po-

[3] See John Malcolm Wallace, "Thomas Traherne and the Structure of Meditation," *ELH*, 25 (1958), 79-89.

etical mode. Alabaster, writing near the end of the 1590's, at the close of the great era of English sonneteering, could use his meditative art to transform the Elizabethan sonnet. Donne, knowing all the devices of current poetry—whether in satire, love song, sonnet, Ovidian elegy, funeral elegy, courtly compliment, or religious hymn—attained his greatest creations in those poems where his mastery of the meditative art could add a new dimension to these modes of poetic art. Herbert, master of music, adept in every form of Elizabethan song or sonnet, could turn all these varied forms into a temple of praise for his Master's presence. And Crashaw, drawn to the extravagant modes of the Continental baroque, could nevertheless, at his best, tame and control his extravaganzas by the firm structure of a meditation.

II

To illustrate this convergence of the arts, let us look closely at one great poem that may be said to represent an epitome of the art of meditation, as Dawson has explained the process. It is Donne's "Hymn to God my God, in my sicknesse," written in 1623 (or perhaps in 1631), when Donne was in his fifties: it is thus a poem that may be regarded as the culmination of a lifetime's practice in the arts of poetry and meditation.

Its opening stanza recalls the careful preparation that preceded meditation: preparation in which the end and aim of the process was fully plotted and foreseen, and in which the speaker placed himself securely in the presence of God:

> Since I am comming to that Holy roome,
> Where, with thy quire of Saints for evermore,
> I shall be made thy Musique; As I come
> I tune the Instrument here at the dore,
> And what I must doe then, thinke here before.

The emphasis falls upon the deliberate process of *thinking:* the meditation will proceed by rational, articulated stages. First comes the "composition of place," in which the speaker, lying upon what he believes will be his deathbed, works out a careful "similitude" that will enable him to understand himself:

> Whilst my Physitians by their love are growne
> Cosmographers, and I their Mapp, who lie
> Flat on this bed, that by them may be showne
> That this is my Southwest discoverie
> *Per fretum febris,* by these streights to die . . .

The doctors are charting forth upon his outstretched body a "discoverie" such as Magellan made; but the "streights" through which this passage will be made are the straits, the difficulties and pains, of death: *Per fretum febris,* "through the straits of fever." The witty play on words shows a remarkable equanimity, that striking ability of Donne to view his own situation from a distance, to hold his own body and soul off at arm's length and study his situation in objective detail, as the art of meditation encouraged one to do.

So Donne sees that he is now upon his westward passage, toward sundown, but as he questions himself, he finds joy in the prospect, for he knows that a flat map is only an illusory diagram. At the far edge, West becomes East, sundown becomes sunrise:

> I joy, that in these straits, I see my West;
> For, though theire currants yeeld returne to none,
> What shall my West hurt me? As West and East
> In all flatt Maps (and I am one) are one,
> So death doth touch the Resurrection.

Donne's questioning in the middle stanzas of the poem indicates a process of analysis bent upon understanding the goal of his passage, and indeed the very questions imply the goal:

Is the Pacifique Sea my home? Or are
The Easterne riches? Is *Jerusalem?*
Anyan, and *Magellan,* and *Gibraltare,*
All streights, and none but streights, are wayes to them,
Whether where *Japhet* dwelt, or *Cham,* or *Sem.*

The traveler to the peaceful ocean, or to the wealth of the Orient, or to that holy city whose name means "Vision of Peace," may move through the "Straits of Anyan" (supposed to separate Asia and America), or the Straits of Magellan, or the Straits of Gibraltar. But however one goes, the voyage is full of pain and difficulty. And this is true whatever regions of the earth he may sail from or sail between, "Whether where *Japhet* dwelt, or *Cham,* or *Sem.*" In thus recalling the ancient division of the earth into the inheritance given to the three sons of Noah, Donne suggests the universality and the inevitability of those straits which face every man who seeks his ultimate home.

In the geography of Donne's present moment there is only one goal, the heavenly Paradise made possible by Calvary, redemption by the sacrifice of Christ. In the outer world this singleness of aim is suggested by the fact that the Paradise of Eden (usually set in Mesopotamia) and Calvary have both been located in the same region of the earth, the Near East. In the same way Adam and Christ now meet in the sick man on his bed. The sweat of his fever fulfills the curse laid upon the first Adam, but the blood of Christ will, the speaker hopes, redeem his soul:

We thinke that *Paradise* and *Calvarie,*
Christs Crosse, and *Adams* tree, stood in one place;
Looke Lord, and finde both *Adams* met in me;
As the first *Adams* sweat surrounds my face,
May the last *Adams* blood my soule embrace.

He prays in familiar colloquy that, for his funeral shroud, he may be wrapped in the blood of Christ, a royal garment of purple, and that thus he may be granted the Crown of Glory in

Heaven. So the poem ends with a recapitulation of the central paradox: death is the passage to life, West and East are one, flatness leads to rising:

> So, in his purple wrapp'd receive mee Lord,
> By these his thornes give me his other Crowne;
> And as to others soules I preach'd thy word,
> Be this my Text, my Sermon to mine owne,
> Therfore that he may raise the Lord throws down.

The closing colloquy reminds us that the whole poem has been spoken in the presence of God: it is all a testimony of faith presented as a hymn of gratitude to the Creator.

The poem, then, reveals in miniature all the essential components of a full religious meditation: preparation, composition, discourse (in the old sense of analytic reasoning), and colloquy; or, to use other terms of the time, memory, understanding, and will, the three powers of the soul which are unified in the process of meditation, forming an interior trinity that represents an image, although defaced, of the greater Trinity. The poem thus becomes the ultimate tuning of that "Instrument" which was John Donne himself: poet, theologian, voyager, preacher, meditative man. If one wonders to find such wit and ingenuity manifested even on the deathbed, the answer is clear: here is the instrument that God has made, and at the last, it is proper that the unique timbre and tone of the instrument should be heard.

III

At the same time this meditative poem is also a work in "the metaphysick style"—the style that in Samuel Johnson's classic account finds its distinctive feature in the witty manipulation of the conceit: "a combination of dissimilar images, or discovery of occult resemblances in things apparently unlike." "The most heterogeneous ideas are yoked by violence together; nature and art are ransacked for illustrations, comparisons, and allusions. . . ." [4] It is worth quoting the familiar words again, since the studies of Mazzeo and Bethell[5] have had the effect of extending, enriching, and giving a positive emphasis to this Johnsonian view, through careful examination of the theories of poetic wit developed on the Continent during the seventeenth century by critical writers such as Gracián and Tesauro. From the standpoint of those contemporary critics, the witty use of the conceit, when properly developed, had a truly metaphysical significance, for it arose from the philosophic doctrine of correspondences. As Mazzeo sums up the view: "Thus God created a world full of metaphors, analogies and conceits, and so far from being ornamentation, they are the law by which creation was effected. God wrote the book of nature in metaphor, and so it should be read. . . . The universe is a vast net of correspondences which unites the whole multiplicity of being. The poet approaches and creates his reality by a series of more or less elaborate correspondences." "God created such a world for the purpose of arousing the wonder of men, and man himself made conceits because he alone of all the creatures of God needed to seek out the variety of the universe and express it." [6]

Readers of the excellent anthologies of metaphysical poetry compiled by Grierson, Miss Gardner, or Frank Warnke[7] will be

[4] See Johnson's Life of Cowley.

[5] See Joseph Anthony Mazzeo, "A Seventeenth-Century Theory of Metaphysical Poetry," and "Metaphysical Poetry and the Poetic of Correspondence," originally published in 1951 and 1953 and now collected in Mazzeo's *Renaissance and Seventeenth-Century Studies* (New York, Columbia University Press, 1964), pp. 29-59. Much the same view has been independently presented by S. L. Bethell, "The Nature of Metaphysical Wit," *Northern Miscellany of Literary Criticism*, 1 (1953), 19-40; more easily available in Frank Kermode's collection, *Discussions of John Donne* (Boston, D. C. Heath & Co., 1962), pp. 136-49.

[6] Mazzeo, *Renaissance and Seventeenth-Century Studies*, pp. 54-6.

[7] *Metaphysical Lyrics and Poems of the Seventeenth Century*, ed. Herbert J. C. Grierson (Oxford, Clarendon Press, 1921); *The Metaphysical Poets*, ed. Helen Gardner (Baltimore, Penguin Books, 1957); *Euro-*

convinced that some such term as "metaphysical" (or *concettismo*) is needed to describe this pervasive poetical style that flourished in England and on the Continent during the seventeenth century. Familiarity with these anthologies may also suggest that the common element serving to join these poems under one cover, and to discriminate them from other types of poetry, lies in the use of the conceit, as described by Miss Gardner: "In a metaphysical poem the conceits are instruments of definition in an argument or instruments to persuade." [8]

In any poetry of argument and persuasion the effect of an actual speaking voice becomes essential; and yet this effect in itself cannot provide a discriminating criterion, since it is also found in Sidney's sonnets, in Ben Jonson and his followers, and of course in the drama of the theater. The voice of living speech is everywhere in the poetry of Donne's time; in discussing poetical modes, we need to ask where the voice is speaking, and to whom, and for what end. When the voice is speaking inwardly, to the self, or to God, or to the self in the presence of God, for the purpose of understanding the self in relation to the divine—then we are in the presence of meditative poetry, which may or may not show the co-presence of "the metaphysick style."

Introspection, self-analysis, the interior drama of the self—this action is not by any means essential to metaphysical poetry, as half the poems usually collected under this label will show. We must distinguish between the meditative and the metaphysical, as Warnke suggests: "For the meditation is a genre—one which recurs at intervals in our history and which, in the sixteenth and seventeenth centuries, assumed a special importance. Metaphysical poetry is a particular style, a historically limited manner of writing in various genres. At the same time, one

---

pean Metaphysical Poetry, ed. Frank J. Warnke (New Haven, Yale University Press, 1961).

[8] Gardner, *Metaphysical Poets*, p. 21.

must recognize the important relationship which this genre and this style bear to one another." [9] I would agree with Warnke that the roots of this relationship lie in the spirit of the age; meditative action and the metaphysical style reflect a kindred response to the same basic conditions.

The metaphysical style of writing arose, it seems, in response to a widespread reaction against the efflorescent, expansive, highly melodious mode of the earlier Renaissance, as found in Edmund Spenser; it arose also, I believe, in response to a widespread feeling that the manifold expansions of human outlook were rapidly moving out of control: expansions through recovery of the classics, through access to the Bible in vernacular languages, through a new emphasis upon the early fathers of the Church, through the advance of science in all areas, and through the vigorous exploration of the earth by seamen, traders, and conquistadors. As a result, in the latter part of the sixteenth century poetry showed a tendency to coalesce and concentrate its powers toward the sharp illumination and control of carefully selected moments in experience.

Metaphysical poems tend to begin abruptly, in the midst of an occasion; and the meaning of the occasion is explored and grasped through a peculiar use of metaphor. The old Renaissance conceit, the ingenious comparison, is developed into a device by which the extremes of abstraction and concreteness, the extremes of unlikeness, may be woven together into a fabric of argument unified by the prevailing force of "wit." *Wit*, in all the rich and varied senses that the word held in this era: intellect, reason, powerful mental capacity, cleverness, ingenuity, intellectual quickness, inventive and constructive ability, a talent for uttering brilliant things, the power of amusing surprise.

The norm of this metaphysical, "conceited" style may be suggested by one of Thomas Carew's poems, "To my inconstant Mistris," a poem that shows the strong influence of Donne:

[9] Warnke, *European Metaphysical Poetry*, p. 56, n. 72.

When thou, poore excommunicate
  From all the joyes of love, shalt see
The full reward, and glorious fate,
  Which my strong faith shall purchase me,
  Then curse thine owne inconstancy.

A fayrer hand than thine, shall cure
  That heart, which thy false oathes did wound;
And to my soul, a soul more pure
  Than thine, shall by Loves hand be bound,
  And both with equall glory crown'd.

Then shalt thou weepe, entreat, complain
  To Love, as I did once to thee;
When all thy teares shall be as vain
  As mine were then, for thou shalt bee
  Damn'd for thy false Apostasie.

The poem is built upon an original use of the familiar conceit by which the experience of human love is rendered in religious terms. Here the faithless lady is excommunicated as an apostate from the religion of love, while her lover will receive the reward of his "strong faith" by being crowned in glory, like the saints in heaven. But, paradoxically, his faith will be demonstrated, his constancy in love rewarded, by the act of turning to another lady, with a "fayrer hand" and "a soul more pure." Inconstancy is thus met with the threat of counter-inconstancy; and all the rich religious terms take on in the end a swagger of bravado. The poem thus presents a brief episode in erotic frustration, a vignette in which the backlash of the lover's bitterness is conveyed by the immediacy of his language, by the conversational flexibility of actual speech working within a strict stanza-form. Here we may see a representative poem in the metaphysical style, composed by a man whose life and works give no evidence of any significant concern with religious meditation.

Now, to see again how the interior discipline of meditation could work within this witty mode of writing, we may look at a sonnet written, it seems, about ten years before John Donne's Holy Sonnets: one of William Alabaster's poems dealing with "the ensignes of Christes Crucifyinge." The sonnet begins with a direct address to the symbols of the Crucifixion, which the speaker appears to have directly before his eyes; crying out to them, fully aware of the paradoxes that they represent, he proposes the question of his own proper response:

> O sweete, and bitter monuments of paine
> bitter to Christ who all the paine endured
> butt sweete to mee, whose Death my life procured
> how shall I full express, such loss, such gaine?

Turning to consider the faculties that lie within himself, his tongue, his eyes, his soul, he proceeds to explain to himself how these may be led toward their proper end, by writing in the book of his soul the record of his sin:

> My tonge shall bee my penne, mine eyes shall raine,
> teares for my Inke, the place where I was cured
> shall bee my booke, where haveing all abjured
> and calling heavens to record in that plaine
> thus plainely will I write, noe sinne like mine;

And finally, holding fast with tenacious logic to his previous images, he closes in colloquy with the Lord, whose presence has been implicit throughout:

> when I have done, doe thou Jesue divine
> take upp the tarte spunge of thy passione
> and blott itt forth: then bee thy spiritt the Quill
> thy bloode the Inke, and with compassione
> write thus uppon my soule: thy Jesue still.

Abrupt opening, condensed and compact phrasing, with touches of colloquial speech, witty development of central conceits, coalescing the abstract and the concrete, logic, paradox—all the qualities of the European metaphysical style are there—yet something more creates the poem's modest success. The speaker has learned how to make himself present before the "monuments" of the Passion, how to concentrate memory, understanding, and will upon these symbols of Christ's suffering, how to develop the personal meaning of the Passion through the use of appropriate similitudes, how to drive home the meaning for the self in affectionate colloquy with God. The art of meditation has provided the techniques by which Alabaster could create a brief interior drama. It is, I believe, in these techniques of self-dramatization that we find the peculiar contribution of the art of meditation to poetry. They are techniques that may combine with a great variety of poetical styles: early Elizabethan, metaphysical, Jonsonian, baroque, or Miltonic.

Thus the ways in which a meditative action may be found in poetry are manifold: no brief definition could hope to hold the adventurous vitality of the meditative art, as changing, resourceful, and elusive as the mind in which the meditation is enacted. Now and then, as in the case of Donne's Hymn, one may say that the poem is a meditation: Donne himself uses the term to describe his fifteenth Holy Sonnet:

> Wilt thou love God, as he thee! then digest,
> My Soule, this wholsome meditation . . .

But, for the most part, it is better to speak of meditative poems, that is to say, poems in which some aspects of the meditative art may be discerned. From this standpoint, a poem such as Marvell's "Dialogue, between the Resolved Soul, and Created Pleasure" might be called meditative, since it enacts an interior drama; but it is not, of course, a meditation of the kind that Dawson describes. One may also, in poets such as Donne or Marvell, find some reflection of meditative habits in poems that are secular ("The Garden") or in poems that are cleverly profane ("The Funerall"). If, as Wallace Stevens suggests, meditation is the mind's "essential exercise," one would expect the results to ramify throughout a poet's career.

IV

This effort to distinguish between the meditative and the metaphysical may help to solve the problem of Donne's relation to later poets of the seventeenth century. Specific debts to Donne are obvious in some of the secular poetry of the period, such as Carew's, but in the religious poetry of Herbert, Crashaw, or Vaughan, where one somehow feels a more essential kinship, such debts are much more elusive, indeed almost nonexistent. To some it has seemed possible to argue that in general Herbert descends from Donne, and that since Herbert influenced Crashaw and Vaughan, the two latter poets are thus at least the grandsons of Donne. But recent studies have shown Herbert's deep-rooted independence of Donne: his use of medieval forms and symbols, his mastery of all varieties of Elizabethan poetry and song, his mastery of the meditative techniques.[10] What Herbert passed on to Vaughan was his own great and original creation, which Vaughan proceeded to use in his own highly original way, combining Herbert's example with the example of the Sons of Ben Jonson, to whose line he displays his allegiance in his early secular poems. The few echoes of Donne that we meet in Vaughan's first volume (1646) are overwhelmed by his dominant experiments in the Jonsonian mode of couplet-rhetoric, as the opening poem of the volume clearly testifies, a poem addressed to a certain friend, R.W.:

> When we are dead, and now, no more
> Our harmles mirth, our wit, and score
> Distracts the Towne; when all is spent
> That the base niggard world hath lent

[10] See Rosemond Tuve, A *Reading of George Herbert* (London, Faber & Faber, 1952); Margaret Bottrall, *George Herbert* (London, John Murray, 1954); Joseph H. Summers, *George Herbert, His Religion and Art* (Cambridge, Harvard University Press, 1954); and my own study, *The Poetry of Meditation*, 2nd edn. (New Haven, Yale University Press, 1962), esp. Chap. 7.

Thy purse, or mine; when the loath'd noise
Of Drawers, Prentises, and boyes
Hath left us, and the clam'rous barre
Items no pints i'th'Moone, or Starre . . .
When all these Mulcts are paid, and I
From thee, deare wit, must part, and dye;
Wee'le beg the world would be so kinde,
To give's one grave, as wee'de one minde;
There (as the wiser few suspect,
That spirits after death affect)
Our soules shall meet, and thence will they
(Freed from the tyranny of clay)
With equall wings, and ancient love
Into the Elysian fields remove,
Where in those blessed walkes they'le find,
More of thy Genius, and my mind:
First, in the shade of his owne bayes,
Great *BEN* they'le see, whose sacred Layes,
The learned Ghosts admire, and throng,
To catch the subject of his Song.
Then *Randolph* in those holy Meades,
His Lovers, and *Amyntas* reads,
Whilst his Nightingall close by,
Sings his, and her owne Elegie;
From thence dismiss'd by subtill roades,
Through airie paths, and sad aboads;
They'le come into the drowsie fields
Of Lethe, which such vertue yeelds,
That (if what Poets sing be true)
The streames all sorrow can subdue.

This steady, terse, and easy handling of the tetrameter couplet is a hallmark of the Jonsonian mode, and it is a form into which many of Vaughan's finest poems in *Silex Scintillans* are cast. Yet poems in the tetrameter couplet are not at all characteristic of Donne or Herbert. It is worth noting, too, in passing, that this Jonsonian use of the tetrameter couplet is found in Crashaw's poems on St. Teresa (along with variations into the pentameter); and it is also one of Andrew Marvell's favorite forms. This does not mean that we should substitute Jonson for Donne as the prime poetical model for these writers; in fact, the influence of Jonson and that of Donne are almost inseparably intermingled throughout the seventeenth century, and particularly in Marvell, the most eclectic of poets. But the appearance of a Jonsonian style in these poets will provide striking evidence of the way in which the art of meditation could and did combine with any available mode in poetry.

To his early practice in the Jonsonian mode, and to the great example of Herbert, Vaughan added the indispensable element: his own powerful mode of Augustinian meditation, probing the memory for glimmerings of the divine light of Eden, never quite lost in man. Thus too with Traherne, who carries to an optimistic extreme the Augustinian conviction that the divine image lies within man's memory, to be uncovered and restored by meditation. Traherne's "Third Century," with its intermingled prose and poetry, provides a particularly clear example of the convergence of the two arts.

Crashaw, though resembling Herbert and Jonson in places, finds his central poetic allegiance in the Continental baroque. The kinship that he truly holds with Donne and Herbert does not lie within poetical traditions, strictly so called; it lies rather in Crashaw's own underlying mastery of the art of meditation, by which he often gives the firm and subtle structure of his "wit of Love" to violent sensory effects that may on the surface seem to escape all reasonable control.

Finally, far away from England, and even farther away, in every respect, from the Italy where Richard Crashaw found his final refuge, the meditative line of the seventeenth century ends with the Puritan Edward Taylor, writing his *Preparatory Meditations* in the wilderness of Massachusetts, before offering the Lord's Supper to his company of the Elect. Taylor's chief poetical models appear to have been Herbert and Quarles, but the rude power of his poetry seems to derive from his command of the traditional method of meditation, adapted to his Puritan beliefs. It is an appropriate tribute to the deep and varied appeal of the art of meditation in this era that its first significant English poet should have been the young Jesuit, Robert Southwell, who returned secretly to his native land after ten years of training by the Counter Reformation, and that the last should have been the Calvinist Taylor, who left England to seek the freedom of his faith in the New World.

IV

Edward Taylor: *Preparatory Meditations*

EDWARD TAYLOR'S major work, *Preparatory Meditations,* is made up of 217 poems, written from 1682 to 1725, while Taylor was serving as minister to the frontier settlement of Westfield, Massachusetts. Since 128 of these Meditations were published for the first time in Donald Stanford's edition of 1960,[1] until then the full range and power of this work had not been manifested; and, as a result, students of Taylor had tended to give at least equal attention to his long doctrinal allegory, *Gods Determinations,* which has been available in its entirety in Thomas Johnson's selection from Taylor's poetry.[2] *Gods Determinations* is a significant work, unique in English poetry; it reveals the workings of the Puritan doctrine of Grace through a framework derived from the old devices of medieval allegory; and it develops, by the blunt insistence of its verse, a certain crude and battering strength. Yet when all is said, *Gods Determinations* remains, I think, a labor of versified doctrine; only a few of its lyrics can approach the best of the *Meditations* in poetical quality. In the end, Taylor's standing as a poet must be measured by a full and careful reading of the *Meditations.*

1 *The Poems of Edward Taylor,* ed. Donald E. Stanford (New Haven, Yale University Press, 1960).

2 *The Poetical Works of Edward Taylor,* ed. Thomas H. Johnson (New York, Rockland Editions, 1939).

Such a reading leaves no doubt that Taylor is a true poet, and yet it is a strange experience, hard to evaluate and explain. For Taylor leads us, inevitably, to compare his achievement with the consummate artistry of George Herbert, whose poetry Taylor echoes throughout the *Meditations,* as well as in his other poems. The example of Herbert appears with special force in the "Prologue," where Taylor five times repeats Herbert's phrase "crumb of dust":

> Lord, Can a Crumb of Dust the Earth outweigh,
> Outmatch all mountains, nay the Chrystall Sky?

It seems a clear echo of Herbert's "The Temper" (I), which also deals with the speaker's sense of inadequacy in attempting the praise of his Lord:

> Wilt thou meet arms with man, that thou dost stretch
> A crumme of dust from heav'n to hell?

And the whole conception of Taylor's poem is perhaps influenced also by a stanza from Herbert's "Longing":

> Behold, thy dust doth stirre,
> It moves, it creeps, it aims at thee:
> Wilt thou deferre
> To succour me,
> Thy pile of dust, wherein each crumme
> Sayes, Come?

The "Prologue" thus prepares us for the strongly Herbertian mode of the first Meditation, with its theme of Love and its familiar exclamations in the presence of the Lord: "Oh! that thy Love might overflow my Heart!" Then, shortly after, we have the three poems that Taylor entitled "The Experience," "The Return," and "The Reflexion"—the only poems in the sequence thus entitled—with their clear reminiscence of the many titles of this kind among Herbert's poetry: "The Answer," "The Reprisall," "The Glance." But these and the other particular echoes of Herbert pointed out in Mr. Stanford's annotations are only the most evident aspects of a pervasive influence. Like Henry Vaughan, Edward Taylor appears to have had a mind saturated with Herbert's poetry, and the result is that a thousand tantalizing echoes of Herbert remain for the most part untraceable because the meditative voice of Herbert has been merged with Taylor's own peculiar voice.

"How sweet a Lord is mine?" "I'le be thy Love, thou my sweet Lord shalt bee." "Then let thy Spirit keepe my Strings in tune." "Blushes of Beauty bright, Pure White, and Red." "My Dear, Deare, Lord I do thee Saviour Call." "What Glory's this, my Lord?" "Oh! Bright! Bright thing! I fain would something say." "Lord speake it home to me, say these are mine." "Oh! that I ever felt what I profess." "What rocky heart is mine?" "Was ever Heart like mine?" "Fain I would sing thy Praise, but feare I feign." "Strang, strang indeed." "I fain would prize and praise thee." "What love, my Lord, dost thou lay out on thine."

> Dull, Dull indeed! What shall it e're be thus?
> And why? Are not thy Promises, my Lord,
> Rich, Quick'ning things? How should my full Cheeks blush
> To finde mee thus? And those a lifeless Word?
> My Heart is heedless: unconcernd hereat:
> I finde my Spirits Spiritless, and flat. [2.12]

All the quotations above are by Taylor; they would not disrupt the harmony of Herbert's *Temple*, and they could be multiplied a hundred times. Yet the full effect of any single poem by Taylor is never quite Herbertian.

Taylor has, first of all, very little of Herbert's metrical skill. In *Gods Determinations* and in the series of short poems on various "occurrants" Taylor attempts to deal with a great variety of stanza forms in Herbert's way, but with only moderate success. In his *Meditations* no such variety is tried: every poem is written in the popular six-line stanza used in Herbert's "Church-porch." Taylor's handling of this stanza seldom rises above competence, and all too often he gives a lame effect of counting syllables and forcing rimes:

> I needed have this hand, that broke off hath
> This Bud of Civill, and of Sacred Faith.

> untill my Virginall
> Chime out in Changes sweet thy Praises shall.

> To view those glories in thy Crown that vapor,
> Would make bright Angells eyes to run a-water.

This sort of clumsiness, in some degree, is found in most of the poems.

Another problem arises when we compare the language of Herbert and Taylor, especially their use of terms from daily speech. As the examples above indicate, Taylor frequently attains the neat and flexible delicacy of Herbert's conversations with God, where the poet speaks in the presence of a familiar friend, as in Herbert's "Easter":

> I got me flowers to straw thy way;
> I got me boughs off many a tree:
> But thou wast up by break of day,
> And brought'st thy sweets along with thee.

This is colloquial, but chastened and restrained: Herbert's language never strays far from the middle way of educated conversation. Herbert was bred in courtly circles, and though he knows that "Kneeling ne'er spoil'd silk stocking," he does not allow slang, dialect, or "low" terms to spoil his neatness. If he allows a line like "The worky-daies are the back-part," this is exceptional: it is at once absorbed into a more discreet context. But consider these lines by Taylor:

> Thus my leane Muses garden thwarts the spring
> Instead of Anthems, breatheth her ahone.
> But duty raps upon her doore for Verse.
> That makes her bleed a poem through her searce. [2.30]

Terms like "ahone" and "searce" bring us up abruptly; they lie outside the mainstream of the language, along with dozens of other terms scattered profusely throughout the poetry: *I'st, bedotcht, brudled, crickling, flur, frim, gastard, glout, keck, painticе, riggalld, skeg, slatch, snick-snarls, tantarrow'd, weddenwise, an hurden haump*. Words like these, whether coinages, phonetic spellings, or Leicestershire dialect, require a sizable glossary, such as that provided at the end of Mr. Stanford's volume. And the problem is compounded by the fact that Taylor's range runs at the same time to the far end of the learned spectrum: *epinicioum, dulcifi'de, enkentrism, enucleate, officine, fistulate, obsignation, aromatize, theanthropie, bituminated*. Even John Donne, who likes to mingle learned and colloquial terms, does not display in his poetry so wide a range as this; and for Herbert, of course, extremes in either direction are to be avoided: he follows Ben Jonson's dictum: "Pure and neat language I love, yet plain and customary."

The problems presented by Taylor's strangely assorted diction are inseparable from a third difficulty: his use of the homeliest images to convey the most sacred and reverend themes. Here again Herbert leads the way, with his "Elixir":

All may of thee partake:
Nothing can be so mean,
Which with his tincture (for thy sake)
Will not grow bright and clean.

A servant with this clause
Makes drudgerie divine:
Who sweeps a room, as for thy laws,
Makes that and th' action fine.

But with Herbert these homely images are handled with a bland understatement, a deft restraint:

You must sit down, sayes Love, and taste my meat:
So I did sit and eat.

And in this love, more then in bed, I rest.

This day my Saviour rose,
And did inclose this light for his:
That, as each beast his manger knows,
Man might not of his fodder misse.
Christ hath took in this piece of ground,
And made a garden there for those
Who want herbs for their wound. ["Sunday"]

Herbert thus succeeds by the total poise of his poem: where every syllable is taut, we cannot doubt the speaker's word. But what shall we say of Taylor's treatment of Jonah as the "type" of Christ?

The Grave him swallow'd down as a rich Pill
Of Working Physick full of Virtue which
Doth purge Death's Constitution of its ill.
And womble-Crops her stomach where it sticks.
It heaves her stomach till her hasps off fly.
And out hee comes Cast up, rais'd up thereby. [2.30]

Or this treatment of the sinner's state?

Mine Heart's a Park or Chase of sins: Mine Head
'S a Bowling Alley. Sins play Ninehole here.
Phansy's a Green: sin Barly breaks in't led.
Judgment's a pingle. Blindeman's Buff's plaid there.
Sin playes at Coursey Parke within my Minde.
My Wills a Walke in which it aires what's blinde. [2.18]

Or this account of the operations of Grace?

Shall things run thus? Then Lord, my tumberill
Unload of all its Dung, and make it cleane.
And load it with thy wealthi'st Grace untill
Its Wheeles do crack, or Axletree complain.
I fain would have it cart thy harvest in,
Before its loosed from its Axlepin. [1.46]

A brief acquaintance with Taylor's poetry might easily lead us to dismiss him as a burlap version of Herbert, a quaint primitive who somehow, despite the Indians, managed to stammer out his rude verses well enough to win the title of "our best Colonial poet." Such a judgment would be utterly wrong. Taylor is not a primitive: he is a subtle, learned man who kept his Theocritus and Origen, his Augustine and Horace, with him in the wilderness. We have the inventory of his library:[3] it would have done credit to a London clergyman, and for one on the Westfield frontier it is all but incredible—until we realize that the Puritan minister of New England did not come to make terms with the wilderness: he came to preserve the Truth in all its purity and wonder. Taylor's Meditations represent a lifelong effort of the inner man to apprehend that Truth.

II

As we read more deeply and more widely in Taylor's poetry, we gradually become aware of the tenacious intelligence that underlies these surface crudities: a bold, probing, adventurous intellect that deliberately tries to bend the toughest matter toward his quest for truth. Consider closely, as a representative example, Meditation 32 of the first series, on the text: "1 Cor. 3.22. Whether Paul or Apollos, or Cephas." We need the whole context of those names: *For all things are yours; whether Paul, or Apollos, or Cephas, or the world, or life, or death, or things present, or things to come; all are yours; and ye are Christ's; and Christ is God's.*

Thy Grace, Deare Lord's my golden Wrack, I finde
    Screwing my Phancy into ragged Rhimes,
Tuning thy Praises in my feeble minde
    Untill I come to strike them on my Chimes.
    Were I an Angell bright, and borrow could
    King Davids Harp, I would them play on gold.

[3] See Johnson's edition of Taylor, pp. 201-20.

> But plung'd I am, my minde is puzzled,
> When I would spin my Phancy thus unspun,
> In finest Twine of Praise I'm muzzled.
> My tazzled Thoughts twirld into Snick-Snarls run.
> Thy Grace, my Lord, is such a glorious thing,
> It doth Confound me when I would it sing.

There is an effect of deliberate roughness here, of struggling for adequate expression, climaxed in the vigorous line: "My tazzled Thoughts twirld into Snick-Snarls run." And now, to work his way out of this ragged state, the speaker in the next two stanzas turns to analyse the meaning of God's Love and Grace in lines that gradually become clear, more harmonious, more fluent:

> Eternall Love an Object mean did smite
> Which by the Prince of Darkness was beguilde,
> That from this Love it ran and sweld with spite
> And in the way with filth was all defilde
> Yet must be reconcild, cleansd, and begrac'te
> Or from the fruits of Gods first Love displac'te.
>
> Then Grace, my Lord, wrought in thy Heart a vent,
> Thy Soft Soft hand to this hard worke did goe,
> And to the Milke White Throne of Justice went
> And entred bond that Grace might overflow.
> Hence did thy Person to my Nature ty
> And bleed through humane Veans to satisfy.

There, in the middle stanza of the poem, the central act of Grace is brought home, with perfect clarity and cadence, to the speaker's mind. As a result, his "Snick-Snarls" disappear, and he bursts forth into spontaneous praise:

> Oh! Grace, Grace, Grace! this Wealthy Grace doth lay
> Her Golden Channells from thy Fathers throne,
> Into our Earthen Pitchers to Convay
> Heavens Aqua Vitae to us for our own.
> O! let thy Golden Gutters run into
> My Cup this Liquour till it overflow.

He pauses, then, to analyse the meaning of these images which have burst out so unexpectedly:

> Thine Ordinances, Graces Wine-fats where
> Thy Spirits Walkes, and Graces runs doe ly
> And Angells waiting stand with holy Cheere
> From Graces Conduite Head, with all Supply.
> These Vessells full of Grace are, and the Bowls
> In which their Taps do run, are pretious Souls.

The term "Ordinances" refers specifically to the sacraments of Communion and Baptism, held by Taylor to be the "Seales of the Covenant of Grace." More generally, the term includes the Decrees and Determinations signified by those sacraments. These are the vats of wine from which Grace runs to save the human soul. Realizing now the immensity and the richness of the gift, the speaker has achieved his wish to "play on gold": Grace conveyed through those "Golden Channells" and "Golden Gutters" has brought to the speaker's soul a "Golden Word":

> Thou to the Cups dost say (that Catch this Wine,)
> This Liquour, Golden Pipes, and Wine-fats plain,
> Whether Paul, Apollos, Cephas, all are thine.
> Oh Golden Word! Lord speake it ore again.
> Lord speake it home to me, say these are mine.
> My Bells shall then thy Praises bravely chime.

The poem, I believe, creates a total effect of rough integrity, moving from a ragged opening to the smooth Herbertian phrasing of the close. The rough phrasing, the colloquialism, the vividly concrete imagery, the Herbertian echoes all play their part in a total pattern. I will not argue that such a control is always present in Taylor's *Meditations:* there is, as I have implied, a frequent clumsiness that has no function; and one cannot defend his excesses in developed imagery, as when he shows the prisoners of sin thus released by "the Blood of thy Covenant":

> And now the Prisoners sent out, do come
> Padling in their Canooes apace with joyes
> Along this blood red Sea, Where joyes do throng . . . [2.78]

But frequently, even in poems with grave flaws, the underlying control is greater than we might at first think, and sometimes the flaws recede into insignificance as the whole poem comes into focus.

At the same time, we must reckon with the fact that the *Meditations* are written in sequences, sometimes with tight links between the poems. The poem we have just considered, for example, is part of a sequence of seven Meditations (1.31-7) written on consecutive aspects of the above-quoted passage from I Corinthians 3:21-3. What I have called the tenacity of Taylor's intelligence is enforced when we realize that these seven Meditations, like the others, were composed at intervals of about two months, and sometimes longer, for Communion Sundays; in this case the poems are dated as follows: 17 February 1688/9; 28 April 1689; 7 July 1689; 25 November 1689; 19 January 1689/90; 16 March 1689/90; and 4 May 1690. These Meditations, then, are the outgrowth of a planned series on sequential texts, running over a period of fifteen months. Longer and more striking sequences appear: the thirty meditations on "Types" that begin Taylor's second series; the subsequent series on the nature, love, and power of Christ (2.31-56), which includes the sequence (2.42-56) associated with a group of fourteen sermons preserved by Taylor under the title *Christographia;* the series (2.102-11) in which Taylor deals with the doctrine of the Lord's Supper; and lastly, the long series on sequential texts from Canticles (2.115-53), running from September 1713 to February 1719.

It is worth noting, too, that Taylor started renumbering his *Meditations* when he began the series of poems on typology—that is to say, on events and personages of the Old Testament that were interpreted as prefigurations of the New Testament.

This would seem to be a clear indication that the 49 opening meditations constitute a unit of some kind. The number 49 is probably significant after the manner of the times; it is the perfect multiple of seven, a number whose significance Taylor celebrates in Meditation 21 of the second series:

> What Secret Sweet Mysterie under the Wing
> Of this so much Elected number lies?

In seventeenth-century thought the number 7 and its multiples signified perfection, and it may be that a meditative quest toward the perfect apprehension of God's Love is the key to this opening series. Certainly Love is its theme, as the opening Meditation declares, foreshadowing the struggle of the whole series toward a joyous realization of this Love:

> Oh! that thy Love might overflow my Heart!
> To fire the same with Love: for Love I would.
> But oh! my streight'ned Breast! my Lifeless Sparke!
> My Fireless Flame! What Chilly Love, and Cold?
> In measure small! In Manner Chilly! See.
> Lord blow the Coal: Thy Love Enflame in mee.

Toward the close of the series, after many expressions of desire and longing, the efforts of the lover come to focus more and more upon the promised glories in Heaven, beginning with Meditation 41, on the text "I go to prepare a Place for you":

> Reason, lie prison'd in this golden Chain,
> Chain up thy tongue, and silent stand a while.
> Let this rich Love thy Love and heart obtain
> To tend thy Lord in all admiring Style.

Then the sequence moves through meditations on the "Throne," the "Crown of Life," the "Crown of Righteousness," the "Crown of Glory," and the "White Raiment," to conclude with a sequence of three poems on the text "Enter thou into the joy of thy Lord." Meditation 48 achieves the assurance of an affectionate realization:

When I, Lord, eye thy Joy, and my Love, small,
My heart gives in: what now? Strange! Sure I love thee!
And finding brambles 'bout my heart to crawl
My heart misgives mee. Prize I ought above thee?
Such great Love hugging them, such small Love, thee!
Whether thou hast my Love, I scarce can see.

Yet when the beamings, Lord, of thy rich Joys,
Do guild my Soule, meethinks I'm sure I Love thee.
They Calcine all these brambly trumperys
And now I'm sure that I prize naught above thee.

And Meditation 49 gives the effect of a formal conclusion, since it offers a sustained prayer for the continued operations of Grace upon his sinful soul:

A Lock of Steel upon my Soule, whose key
The serpent keeps, I fear, doth lock my doore.
O pick't: and through the key-hole make thy way
And enter in: and let thy joyes run o're.

Thus, as the full effect of an individual Meditation often enfolds and sustains a number of flaws in detail, so a weak poem may be enfolded and sustained by the part it plays in a developing sequence. The flaws are there, and we do not overlook them; yet the poems, in the large, succeed in creating a highly original world, designed upon a special plan. It is a world where the Puritan doctrine of Grace operates to consecrate, within the soul of one of the Elect, every object, every word, every thought that passes through his anguished, grateful, loving mind. To understand the workings of that world, we need to explore the meaning of that key word which Taylor repeated in his titles more than two hundred times: "meditation."

III

For a Puritan minister of New England in the year 1682, the word "meditation" would have retained, certainly, some of the grimmer implications that it held among the older generation of Puritan ministers, for whom the word signified, primarily, a rigorous self-examination designed to uncover the sins of fallen man. The eminent Connecticut divine Thomas Hooker, for example, devotes seventy-five pages of his treatise *The Application of Redemption* (London, 1657) to a vigorous exhortation toward the "Meditation of sins" as "a special means to break the heart of a sinner" (pp. 208-83). Meditation, he declares, "is as it were the register and remembrancer, that looks over the records of our daily corruptions, and keeps them upon file." Moreover, "Meditation is that which encreaseth the weight of the evil of sin, presseth it down upon the Conscience, and burdens the heart with it until it break under it. It gleans up, and rakes together al the particulars, adds dayly to the load, and laies on until the Axletree split asunder, and the heart fails and dies away under the apprehension of the dreadfulness of the evil." Thus "daily meditation flings in one terror after another," "holds the heart upon the rack under restless and unsupportable pressures," with the result that "the sinner is forced to walk and talk with [sin], to wake and sleep with it, to eat and drink his sins." In this way, "by serious meditation we sew them all up together, we look back to the linage and pedegree of our lusts, and track the abominations of our lives, step by step, until we come to the very nest where they are hatched and bred, even of our original corruption" (pp. 208, 212-13, 219, 221, 271).

But in Edward Taylor's day other aspects of the word "meditation" were operating in Puritan circles, aspects that served to modify and ameliorate the rigor of the older generation. The clearest indication of these newer tendencies, I think, may be found by turning to the most important Puritan treatise on meditation written during the seventeenth century, the fourth part of Richard Baxter's famous work *The Saints Everlasting Rest* (London, 1650). Baxter's works were well known in New England; Taylor's own library contained two of Baxter's treatises, although the *Everlasting Rest* is not one of them. We should recall, too, that Taylor did not leave England until 1668, when he was about the age of 25; he was already highly educated and apparently designed for the ministry; he is said to have attended Cambridge University, and he was at once admitted to Harvard with advanced standing. Taylor, then, came to maturity in England at just the time when the temporary victory of the Puritan Commonwealth had released into new areas the powerful energies of English Puritanism, long constricted by the fierce struggle for survival.

Baxter's treatise on meditation is one of many signs that English Puritanism, in its mid-century moment of dominance, was reaching out into areas hitherto neglected: the place of the mystical Platonist Peter Sterry as Cromwell's chaplain and the presence of John Milton and Andrew Marvell in the inner circles of Cromwell's government will testify to the rich expansion of outlook that occurred in this brief interval. Richard Baxter's treatise, with ten editions appearing in the years 1650-70, played its part in this development by urging Puritans to undertake what his title page calls "the Diligent Practice of that Excellent unknown Duty of *Heavenly Meditation*"—formal meditation on the joys of Heaven. A brief account of Baxter's mode of meditation will help to show how closely Taylor's poetry accords with the expanding outlook of contemporary Puritanism.

Puritanism, of course, was never the solid phalanx of rigorous doctrine that our studies sometimes make it appear: there were always flexible spirits, always exceptions, always examples in earlier Puritans of the kind of advice that Baxter formulated and brought forward into a central influence. Baxter himself cites some of his predecessors to justify his arguments for a different kind of meditation. But when Baxter says that this way of meditation is "unknown" among his people, we may believe that in general he is right: it is impossible to find a shrewder or a better-informed witness.

Meditation in his sense of the term, Baxter declares, is "unknown" among his people largely because they have spent so much time in running "from Sermon to Sermon," or in examining their souls for "signs of their sincerity," or in passively awaiting the gift of "Enthusiastick Consolations" (Pt. IV, pp. 5, 147; I quote from the London edition of 1653). Baxter is clearly attempting to add another dimension to the state of mind that Perry Miller has acutely described in the second chapter of *The New England Mind: The Seventeenth Century*, where he deals with that "unceasing self-examination" by which the Puritan attempted to assure himself that he was indeed regenerated, sanctified, elected. To be sure, the word "meditation" is well known and often used among these people, but, Baxter says, they do not understand its true meaning: "They have thought that Meditation is nothing but the bare thinking on Truths, and the rolling of them in the understanding and memory" (IV, 151). And no one, he notes, in a passage that may bear a special import for the study of Taylor's poetry, no one is more prone to this error than "those that are much in publick duty, especially Preachers of the Gospel."

O how easily may they be deceived here, while they do nothing more then reade of Heaven, and study of Heaven, and preach of Heaven, and pray, and talk of Heaven? what, is not this the Heavenly Life? O that God would reveal to our hearts the danger of this snare! Alas, all this is but meer preparation: This is not the life we speak of, but it's indeed a necessary help thereto. I entreat every one of my Brethren in the Ministry, that they search, and watch against this Temptation: Alas, this is but gathering the materials, and not the erecting of the building it self; this is but gathering our Manna for others, and not eating and digesting our selves. . . . [IV, 122]

And therefore Baxter says to all his people: "this is the great task in hand, and this is the work that I would set thee on; to get these truths from thy head to thy heart, and that all the Sermons which thou hast heard of Heaven, and all the notions that thou hast conceived of this Rest, may be turned into the bloud and spirits of Affection, and thou maist feel them revive thee, and warm thee at the heart" (IV, 151).

Taylor's *Meditations* seem to bear exactly this relation to his sermons, as his full title makes clear: "Preparatory Meditations before my Approach to the Lords Supper. Chiefly upon the Doctrin preached upon the Day of administration." Norman Grabo, in his edition of Taylor's *Christographia*,[4] shows how sermon and Meditation correspond, bearing the same dates and, with one exception, the same biblical texts. The sermon prepares the ground, the doctrine, for the Meditation; while the act of meditation in turn prepares the preacher to receive and administer the sacrament, and to deliver his sermon on that day with "the bloud and spirits of Affection." These poems, then, are properly called *Preparatory Meditations* (not *Sacramental Meditations*, as they used to be called, after a title added by another hand above Taylor's own title): they preserve, in the finest verbal form that Taylor could give, his efforts "to get these truths" from his head to his heart.

Baxter, in a long exposition, makes clear every aspect of the art of meditation as he wished his people to practice it. The method is essentially the same as that which had been advocated, over the preceding century, by Catholic handbooks of devotion. It consists of three essential acts, corresponding to the old division of the faculties or "powers" of the soul into memory, understanding, and will. Thus the work of meditation, for Baxter, proceeds by "the set and solemn acting of all the powers of the soul" (IV, 146). This meditation, he explains, is "set and solemn" because it is performed "when a Christian observing it as a standing duty, doth resolvedly practise it in a constant course" (IV, 153). First, he directs, "you must by *cogitation* go to the Memory (which is the Magazine or Treasury of the Understand-

[4] Edward Taylor, *Christographia*, ed. Norman S. Grabo (New Haven, Yale University Press, 1962).

ing); thence you must take forth those *heavenly doctrines*, which you intend to make the subject of your *Meditation.*" Then, after "you have fetcht from your memory the *matter* of your *Meditation*, your next work is to present it to your *Judgment:* open there the case as fully as thou canst" (IV, 186-7). He has explained earlier that the "great Instrument that this Work is done by, is Ratiocination, Reasoning the case with your selves, Discourse of mind, Cogitation, or Thinking; or, if you will, call it Consideration." This consideration, he declares, "doth, as it were, open the door, between the Head and the Heart" (IV, 178-9).

He particularly urges that the work of consideration be carried on by means of "Soliloquy," "which is nothing but a pleading the case with our own Souls," or, he adds, "a Preaching to ones self." "Why thus must thou do in thy *Meditation* to quicken thy own *heart:* Enter into a serious debate with it: Plead with it in the most moving and affecting language: Urge it with the most weighty and powerful *Arguments*" (IV, 209-10). And so, through the vigorous use of the understanding, the soul is aroused to feel the affections (emotions or feelings) of the will, which, according to Baxter, should be developed in a certain order: love, desire, hope, courage (resolution), and, lastly, joy.

I believe that anyone who reads carefully through the first 49 Meditations of Edward Taylor will quickly sense how closely the poetry accords with such advice by Baxter. It is not essential, of course, to believe that Taylor learned this mode of meditation from Baxter's treatise. By 1682 Baxter's influence had been widely disseminated throughout English Puritanism; and during Taylor's youth in England exhortations to this kind of meditation were available in Catholic or Anglo-Catholic treatises. The chief point is that both Baxter and Taylor, while maintaining all the central Puritan tenets, were participating in one of the central movements of religious devotion in the seventeenth century.

The entire process is accompanied by two other elements which are, in Baxter's view, essential to success in meditation, and are of the utmost importance for Taylor's poetry. The first of these is prayer: requests to God "may be intermixed or added, and that as a very part of the duty it self." Such constant prayer, Baxter says, "keeps the Soul in mind of the *Divine Presence;* it tends also exceedingly to quicken and raise it; so that as God is the highest Object of our *Thoughts,* so our viewing of him, and our speaking to him, and pleading with him, doth more elevate the soul, and actuate the affections, then any other part of *Meditation* can do" (IV, 214).

And secondly, we have the advice stressed by Kenneth Murdock in the second chapter of his study *Literature and Theology in Colonial New England.* As one is aided by the upward looks of prayer, so the meditative man may be constantly aided by downward looks: the senses themselves should be used "to make your *thoughts* of *Heaven* to be piercing, affecting, raising *thoughts.*" The time has come, Baxter believes, for Puritanism to moderate its mistrust of sensory aids in the service of religion. "Why sure it will be a point of our Spiritual prudence, and a singular help to the furthering of the work of Faith, to call in our Sense to its assistance . . . Sure it is both possible and lawful, yea, and necessary too, to do something in this kind; for God would not have given us either our senses themselves, or their usual objects, if they might not have been serviceable to his own Praise, and helps to raise us up to the apprehension of higher things" (IV, 216-17). Following the lead of Scriptural imagery, we must make every effort to apprehend the joys of heaven with our senses: "get the liveliest Picture of them in thy minde that possibly thou canst; meditate of them, as if thou were all the while beholding them, and as if thou were even hearing the *Hallelujahs,* while thou art thinking of them; till thou canst say, Methinks I see a glimpse of the Glory! Methinks I hear the shouts of Joy and Praise!" (IV, 220-21). And he continues for twenty more pages to suggest various ways in which sensory objects and personal experiences may be used constantly "to quicken your affections, by comparing the unseen delights of Heaven, with those smaller which you have seen, and felt in the flesh" (IV, 242).

IV

In Baxter's arguments for the use of sensory images in meditation we have, I believe, the grounds of justification for Taylor's bold and often unseemly use of common imagery. For Baxter's support of this way of meditation is thoroughly and vehemently argued: "He that will speak to mans understanding must speak in mans language, and speak that which he is capable to conceive." "Go to then," he exclaims, "When thou settest thy self to meditate on the joyes above, think on them boldly as Scripture hath expressed them. Bring down thy conceivings to the reach of sense, Excellency without familiarity, doth more amaze then delight us: Both Love and Joy are promoted by familiar acquaintance" (IV, 218-19). Baxter is speaking at this point particularly of meditation upon the Everlasting Rest in Heaven; but he points out elsewhere (IV, 208) that the same methods may be used "for the acting of the contrary and more mixed passions"—such as "hatred and detestation of sin," grief, shame, repentance, and so on.

The whole of the spiritual life, then, is to be apprehended in sensory and colloquial terms. Everything that exists may be used to promote this "familiar acquaintance": thus Taylor uses a rolling pin, roast mutton, a bowling alley, a "Bucking tub," a "Titimouses Quill," milk pails, a "Drippen pan," a "Dish clout," a "Trough of Washing-Swill." "Nothing that is available in human experience is to be legislated out of poetry," says R. P. Warren in a classic essay of modern criticism;[5] Edward Taylor clearly agrees. Are we searching for the nature of Love? Here is the way to bring it home to the heart:

O! what a thing is Love? who can define
    Or liniament it out? Its strange to tell.
A Sparke of Spirit empearld pill like and fine
    In't shugard pargings, crusted, and doth dwell
    Within the heart, where thron'd, without Controle
    It ruleth all the Inmates of the Soule.

It makes a poother in its Secret Sell
    Mongst the affections: oh! it swells, its paind,
Like kirnells soked untill it breaks its Shell
    Unless its object be obtained and gain'd.
    Like Caskd wines jumbled breake the Caske, this Sparke
    Oft swells when crusht: untill it breakes the Heart. [2.66]

Or perhaps we are searching for a way to drive home the horrors of sin:

My Sin! my Sin, My God, these Cursed Dregs,
    Green, Yellow, Blew streakt Poyson hellish, ranck,
Bubs hatcht in natures nest on Serpents Eggs,
    Yelp, Cherp and Cry; they set my Soule a Cramp.
    I frown, Chide, strik and fight them, mourn and Cry
    To Conquour them, but cannot them destroy.

I cannot kill nor Coop them up: my Curb
    'S less than a Snaffle in their mouth: my Rains
They as a twine thrid, snap: by hell they're spurd:
    And load my Soule with swagging loads of pains.
    Black Imps, young Divells, snap, bite, drag to bring
    And pick mee headlong hells dread Whirle Poole in.
[1.39]

As these examples indicate, Taylor has a way of shifting impetuously from image to image in his effort to define and bring

[5] Robert Penn Warren, "Pure and Impure Poetry," in his *Selected Essays* (New York, Random House, 1958), p. 26.

home the spiritual import; in the above four stanzas the images work without confusion, but elsewhere, as earlier critics of Taylor have noted, he jumps from image to image in a way that tends to shake the poem apart: Meditation 37 in the first series will provide examples of this weakness. But a more serious flaw in Taylor's handling of imagery seems to arise from the opposite tendency: he frequently hangs on to an image until he has strained it by excessive ingenuity: Meditation 38 in the first series seems to me an example of this sort of excess.

Yet when all his flaws in dealing with imagery have been acknowledged, even at his worst he retains an attractive vigor; and at his best he can produce an analysed image of a subtlety that equals Herbert:

> I have no plea mine Advocate to give:
>   What now? He'l anvill Arguments greate Store
> Out of his Flesh and Blood to make thee live.
>   O Deare bought Arguments: Good pleas therefore.
>   Nails made of heavenly Steel, more Choice than gold
>   Drove home, Well Clencht, eternally will hold. [1.39]

Thus the nails driven through the flesh of Christ on the Cross are made to symbolize the certainty, as well as the means, of Christ's effective advocacy.

At other times the casual introduction of a homely image or expression is enough to give life to a passage that seems doomed to dryness; thus Taylor deals with Joseph as a Type of Christ:

> Is Josephs glorious shine a Type of thee?
>   How bright art thou? He Envi'de was as well.
> And so was thou. He's stript, and pick't, poore hee,
>   Into the pit. And so was thou. They shell
>   Thee of thy Kirnell. He by Judah's sold
>   For twenty Bits, thirty for thee he'd told.
>
> Joseph was tempted by his Mistress vile.
>   Thou by the Divell, but both shame the foe.

Joseph was cast into the jayle awhile.
And so was thou. Sweet apples mellow so. [2.7]

Sweet apples mellow so. One can endure a good deal of Taylor's clumsiness for one such effect of "familiar acquaintance."

But in the final analysis the success of Taylor's homely images and earthy language must depend on how they function in the whole poem. Here again, I believe, the meditative discipline that lies behind and within the poetry has enabled Taylor to give many of his poetical meditations a firm and operative structure. For the most part, his Meditations are working at the achieved level of the affections. Like the "Divine Meditations" (Holy Sonnets) of John Donne, the sonnets of Gerard Manley Hopkins, or the poems of George Herbert, Taylor's Meditations represent the peaks and pinnacles of the meditative process on which the poet's spiritual life is based:

And now his shining Love beams out its rayes
My Soul, upon thy Heart to thaw the same:
To animate th'Affections till they blaze;
To free from Guilt, and from Sins Slough, and Shame.
Open thy Casement wide, let Glory in,
To Guild thy Heart to be an Hall for him.

My Breast, be thou the ringing Virginalls:
Ye mine Affections, their sweet Golden Strings,
My Panting Heart, be thou for Stops, and Falls:
Lord, let thy quick'ning Beams dance o're the Pins. [1.18]

But at the same time this music of the affections will frequently, and indeed usually, reflect in some measure the stages by which the soul has reached such a level of religious experience. Consequently, in Taylor's meditative poems, as in Donne's or Herbert's or Hopkins', we can often trace clearly, preserved in miniature, the whole process of a meditation, in Baxter's meaning of the term. One example must serve: Meditation 29 of the first series, on the text: "Joh. 20.17. My Father, and your Father, to my God, and your God." The context is important, for the words are spoken by the risen Jesus in the garden of the sepulcher, after Mary Magdalene has mistaken him for the gardener; the garden of the Gospel has provided Taylor with a setting from which the hand of meditation can draw forth from the memory the following vivid picture:

> My shattred Phancy stole away from mee,
> (Wits run a Wooling over Edens Parke)
> And in Gods Garden saw a golden Tree,
> Whose Heart was All Divine, and gold its barke.
> Whose glorious limbs and fruitfull branches strong
> With Saints, and Angells bright are richly hung.

With the situation thus firmly established, consideration then projects the speaker's own plight upon the scene, and explains, with careful analysis, the exact relation of Man to God by developing the central image of a "Grafft" upon that Tree.

> Thou! thou! my Deare-Deare Lord, art this rich Tree
> The Tree of Life Within Gods Paradise.
> I am a Withred Twig, dri'de fit to bee
> A Chat Cast in thy fire, Writh off by Vice.
> Yet if thy Milke white-Gracious Hand will take mee
> And grafft mee in this golden stock, thou'lt make mee.
>
> Thou'lt make me then its Fruite, and Branch to spring.
> And though a nipping Eastwinde blow, and all
> Hells Nymps with spite their Dog's sticks thereat ding
> To Dash the Grafft off, and it's fruits to fall,
> Yet I shall stand thy Grafft, and Fruits that are
> Fruits of the Tree of Life thy Grafft shall beare.
>
> I being grafft in thee there up to stand
> In us Relations all that mutuall are.
> I am thy Patient, Pupill, Servant, and
> Thy Sister, Mother, Doove, Spouse, Son, and Heire.
> Thou art my Priest, Physician, Prophet, King,
> Lord, Brother, Bridegroom, Father, Ev'ry thing.

I being grafft in thee am graffted here
Into thy Family, and kindred Claim
To all in Heaven, God, Saints, and Angells there.
I thy Relations my Relations name.
Thy Father's mine, thy God my God, and I
With Saints, and Angells draw Affinity.

Reason has opened the case as fully as it can, and the door between the head and the heart now stands ajar: the poem concludes with a surge of the affections toward gratitude and praise:

My Lord, what is it that thou dost bestow?
The Praise on this account fills up, and throngs
Eternity brimfull, doth overflow
The Heavens vast with rich Angelick Songs.
How should I blush? how Tremble at this thing,
Not having yet my Gam-Ut, learnd to sing.

But, Lord, as burnish't Sun Beams forth out fly
Let Angell-Shine forth in my Life out flame,
That I may grace thy gracefull Family
And not to thy Relations be a Shame.
Make mee thy Grafft, be thou my Golden Stock.
Thy Glory then I'le make my fruits and Crop.

V

Some readers will no doubt prefer to describe the action of this analysed conceit as "metaphysical" or, perhaps, "baroque." I do not mean to quarrel with these terms, both well established in critical discussion, and each with its own particular use. I must confess, however, that both seem less accurate than the term "meditative," when applied to Taylor's *Preparatory Meditations*. For Baxter's kind of meditation is, like poetry, a verbal action developed through every resource that language can offer.

Near the close of his treatise Baxter sets forth an elementary

"Example" of a full meditation "for the help of the unskilful." This is written in concrete, colloquial, highly charged language which in places sounds like Taylor's poetry—or even like Herbert's poetry—turned into prose:

What thinkest thou, O my Soul, of this most blessed state? What! Dost thou stagger at the *Promise of God* through unbelief? . . . Can *God* lie? or he that is the *Truth* it self, be false? Foolish wretch! What need hath God to flatter thee, or deceive thee? why should he promise thee more then he will perform? Art thou not his *Creature?* a little crumb of dust? [IV, 259]

One might hesitate to attribute that phrase "crumb of dust" to a memory of Herbert, were it not for the fact that later in the meditation (IV, 278) we find Baxter quoting a whole stanza from "*Herberts Poems,* The Glance," and three pages after this, Herbert's entire poem "Dotage," and ten pages after this, a stanza (considerably altered) from Herbert's "Mans medley." Then, after a few pages of concluding advice, Baxter places at the very end of his volume "A Poem of Master G. Herbert; In His Temple": one of Herbert's longest poems, covering three pages here—the poem "Home":

Come dearest Lord; pass not this holy season;
My flesh and bones and joynts do pray;
And even my verse, when by the rhyme and reason
The word is, Stay, say's ever, Come.
O shew thy self to me,
Or take me up to thee.

Thus Baxter himself indicates how meditation and poetry converge. Baxter, Herbert, The Psalms, the Canticles—these are enough to suggest the literary traditions which made it possible for Edward Taylor to compose his poetical meditations in the wilderness. They will suggest, too, Taylor's place in literary history as the last heir of the great tradition of English meditative poetry that arose in the latter part of the sixteenth century, with

Robert Southwell as its first notable example, continued on through the religious poetry of John Donne (and also in those of his secular poems that have meditative elements), reached a fulfillment in the *Temple* of George Herbert, went abroad to include the baroque motifs of Richard Crashaw, found another home in Henry Vaughan's uneven but inspired meditations on the "creatures," strengthened the fiber of Andrew Marvell's slender muse, and, so far as England was concerned, died at the death of Thomas Traherne in 1674, with both his prose meditations and their companionate poems unpublished. But as Crashaw had gone abroad to preserve and extend his Catholic allegiance, so, at the end of the line, in 1668, Edward Taylor sailed for New England, and there, surrounded by the rude and dangerous life of the frontier, composed his Puritan and meditative poems.

What I have said thus far has been concerned with enforcing Taylor's relation to the traditions of English culture. Is there anything in Taylor's poetry that could be called distinctively American? In the whole large range of his *Preparatory Meditations* and *Gods Determinations*, there is almost nothing (except for an occasional canoe or rattlesnake) that one could single out to suggest a specifically American allusion. In some ways Edward Taylor may seem to bear out the charge brought against New England Puritanism by William Carlos Williams in his *In the American Grain* (pp. 110f.): that the Puritans refused to *touch* —that they set up a "resistance to the wilderness"—"with a ground all blossoming about them." Williams speaks of the "rigid clarity" of their religion, "its *inhuman* clarity, its steel-like thrust from the heart of each isolate man straight into the tabernacle of Jehovah without embellishment or softening." "Its firmness is its beauty . . . Its virtue is to make each man stand alone, surrounded by a density as of the Lord: a seed in its shell." It is true that, so far as local allusion is concerned, Taylor's *Med-*

itations, one might think, could as well have been written in England—or in India, or in Egypt.

Yet the fact remains that no such poetry was being written in the England of Taylor's day; and indeed, poetry with Taylor's peculiar quality could not, I think, have been written at all in England, even by Taylor himself. For the writer in England, wherever he may be living, works within a certain conditioning imposed by the context of that intimate island's culture: he knows the ways of other learned, literary men; he senses the current modes of writing; and even though he believes in freedom of language, as Baxter does, the writer is nevertheless tacitly and unconsciously influenced by the accepted conventions of public speech and writing in that culture. George Herbert lived in Bemerton, a country parson, and yet he could walk from there to the high and ancient culture of Salisbury. But in Taylor's frontier settlement these guide-lines fall away; cultivated conversation becomes rare; the minister's work is solely occupied with humble folk; his daily life is rude, simple, concerned with the bare, stark facts of survival in a village that is at times little more than a stockade. Even the intellectual life must be limited to theology and the classics; Taylor's library at his death contained only one work of English poetry: the poems of Anne Bradstreet.

Thus the poet's conversations with God are spoken in a language that the meditative poet, living in England, would never use. For the soul, in meditation, is to speak as the man himself has come to speak; any other language would be dishonest and pretentious. So Taylor speaks in this peculiar mixture of the learned and the rude, the abstract and the earthy, the polite and the vulgar; for such distinctions do not exist in the wilderness.

The result is often lame and crude; in some respects the writer needs the support and guidance of an established culture; but since he in himself is almost the sole bearer and creator of whatever culture his village will possess, he must do what he can with whatever materials lie at hand. Out of his very deficiencies he creates a work of rugged and original integrity. The result helps to mark the beginning of an American language, an American literature.

V

Whitman and Dickinson:
Two Aspects of the Self

EXCEPT for a shared inheritance of Emersonian thought, which they put to quite different uses, Walt Whitman and Emily Dickinson have very little in common, whether in their personal lives or in their poetical manner. One thinks of the portrait of Walt in the first edition of *Leaves of Grass:* open-shirted, slouching, "one of the roughs"; Walt the printer, reporter, and newspaper editor, Walt the traveler to New Orleans and the Great Lakes, Walt the hospital attendant, moving among the wounded soldiers of the Civil War. And then one thinks of Emily, spending nearly all her days in Amherst, spending indeed the last twenty years of her life almost entirely within the confines of her father's yard, dressed in white, and sending forth her "letter to the World/That never wrote to Me." We think of the long, loping, irregular lines of Whitman, his endless catalogues, his boundless inclusiveness:

> A Kentuckian walking the vale of the Elkhorn in my deer-skin
>   leggings, a Louisianian or Georgian,
> A boatman over lakes or bays or along coasts, a Hoosier,
>   Badger, Buckeye;
> At home on Kanadian snow-shoes or up in the bush, or with
>   fishermen off Newfoundland,
> At home in the fleet of ice-boats, sailing with the rest and
>   tacking,

At home on the hills of Vermont or in the woods of Maine,
or the Texan ranch . . .
A farmer, mechanic, artist, gentleman, sailor, quaker,
Prisoner, fancy-man, rowdy, lawyer, physician, priest.[1]

And we think of Emily's clipped and rigorous selectivity:

The Soul selects her own Society—
Then—shuts the Door—
To her divine Majority—
Present no more—

* * * * *

I've known her—from an ample nation—
Choose One—
Then—close the Valves of her attention—
Like Stone—

These are the representations of two utterly different modes of poetry, each in its own way trying to find an answer to the problems of a world and a self hovering between dissolution and creation. Indeed, the external struggle of the Civil War and the internal struggle of the poets might be said to have their roots in much the same issue: a turbulent originality of purpose, unable any longer to accept the traditional modes of life and thought, struggling to create a new world: "The Modern Man I sing."

Surely no one was ever more thoroughly aware of his originality than Walt Whitman: he throws away the stanzas and the rhymes of traditional poetry; he refuses even to use the customary names of the months, calling them, in Biblical, Quaker fashion, Third-month or Fifth Month: the national holiday becomes "the fourth of Seventh-month." He insists on bringing into poetry materials hardly regarded as "poetic" in his day: the butcher-boy in his killing-clothes, the bus driver "with his inter-

[1] With a few exceptions my quotations from Whitman are taken from the text of 1891-2 as presented in *The Collected Writings of Walt Whitman: Leaves of Grass*, Comprehensive Reader's Edition, ed. Harold W. Blodgett and Sculley Bradley (New York University Press, 1965).

rogating thumb," the clam-digger tucking in his trouser-ends, the fare-collector going through the train, giving notice "by the jingling of loose change," picnics, and jigs, and a game of baseball, triphammers, fire-engines, stevedores, and sign-painters. He uses colloquial, archaic, or invented language unknown to the poetry of his time: "the blab of the pave," "my gore dribs," "rock me in billowy drowse," "flatting the flesh of my nose," the "limpsy" slave, "to dicker," "shoulder your duds," and "rest the chuff of your hand on my hip." It is all, as he proudly says, part of "my gab" and "my barbaric yawp."

Yet with all his exuberant originality, Whitman, like every poet, has his ancestors. We may feel them present in the long, rhythmic, flowing, unrhymed verses, in the parallel phrasing, in the frequent linking of lines by *and:*

And I know that the hand of God is the promise of my own,
And I know that the spirit of God is the brother of my own,
And that all the men ever born are also my brothers, and the women my sisters and lovers. . . .

I am the poet of the Body and I am the poet of the Soul,
The pleasures of heaven are with me and the pains of hell are with me,
The first I graft and increase upon myself, the latter I translate into a new tongue.

Whether in manner or in substance, there seems to be only one essential precedent for such writing—the prophetic poetry of the Bible, particularly the prophetic books of the Old Testament, which Whitman knew thoroughly.

There has been of late a considerable tendency to deny the validity of the term "prophetic poetry" to Whitman's best work, although Whitman himself clearly aligned his poetry with this kind of writing. Thus in *Democratic Vistas* (1871) he proclaimed the need for a "prophetic literature of these States" and warned his countrymen: "If you would have greatness, know that you must conquer it through ages, centuries—must pay for it with a proportionate price. For you too, as for all lands, the struggle, the traitor, the wily person in office, scrofulous wealth, the surfeit of prosperity, the demonism of greed, the hell of passion, the decay of faith, the long postponement, the fossil-like lethargy, the ceaseless need of revolutions, prophets, thunder-storms, deaths, births, new projections and invigorations of ideas and men." [2] It has been argued that Whitman's conception of himself as a prophet was indeed the downfall of his poetry, as he came more and more to develop what he calls humorously, in "Song of Myself," "my prophetical screams." That is—so the charge runs—his tendency to make abstract assertions about the future grew, until he weakened his essential poetical power, his ability to deal concretely and dynamically with the world about him.

No doubt these charges against Whitman are true, except for some of the Civil War poems. I share the preference of many critics for the early editions of 1855 or 1860, as against the many revisions, rearrangements, and additions that Whitman made up to the time of his death in 1892. It is dangerous for a poet to allow himself to say, as Whitman says in one of the later poems ("Shut Not Your Doors"): "The words of my book nothing, the drift of it every thing," for a poet to whom words have become nothing does indeed run the risk that Whitman humorously prophesies in "Song of Myself," when he cries, "My ties and ballasts leave me." His "flights of a fluid and swallowing soul" may fly out too often beyond the human horizon, into a place where the air is too thin for poetry. But all this has nothing to do with the question of whether Whitman's poetry at its best deserves to be called *prophetic*.

To grasp Whitman's essential relation to the Biblical Prophets, we must keep in mind the original meaning of the word

[2] *The Collected Writings of Walt Whitman: Prose Works 1892*, ed. Floyd Stovall (2 vols., New York University Press, 1963-4), II, 416, 423.

"prophet." For the prophet was not simply one who foretold the future; he was, in the old Greek meaning of the word, one who speaks for another—specifically, one who speaks for God and interprets the divine will to man. Thus we have the refrain of Ezekiel, "And the word of the Lord came unto me, saying . . ." Or in Jeremiah and Isaiah—"Thus saith the Lord." When the Hebrew prophets interpret the future, it is for the purpose of arousing their people to the needs and demands of the present, it is to exhort and warn their people that they must fulfill their faith now, be constant to their trust now, be true now to their appointed part in the divine mission. To convey that urgent, immediate sense of mission, the prophet's imagination reaches forth over the whole known world, comprehending in detail the life of the time in vast visions of creation and destruction, as in Ezekiel's great vision of the doomed wealth and power of Tyre:

Tarshish was thy merchant by reason of the multitude of all kind of riches; with silver, iron, tin, and lead, they traded in thy fairs.

Javan, Tubal, and Meshech, they were thy merchants: they traded the persons of men and vessels of brass in thy market.

They of the house of Togarmah traded in thy fairs with horses and horsemen and mules.

The men of Dedan were thy merchants; many isles were the merchandise of thine hand: they brought thee for a present horns of ivory and ebony.

Syria was thy merchant by reason of the multitude of the wares of thy making: they occupied in thy fairs with emeralds, purple, and broidered work, and fine linen, and coral, and agate.

Judah, and the land of Israel, they were thy merchants: they traded in thy market wheat of Minnith, and Pannag, and honey, and oil, and balm.

Damascus was thy merchant in the multitude of the wares of thy making, for the multitude of all riches; in the wine of Helbon, and white wool.

Dan also and Javan going to and fro occupied in thy fairs: bright iron, cassia, and calamus, were in thy market.

* * * * *

Haran, and Canneh, and Eden, the merchants of Sheba, Asshur, and Chilmad, were thy merchants.
These were thy merchants in all sorts of things, in blue clothes, and broidered work, and in chests of rich apparel, bound with cords, and made of cedar, among thy merchandise.

We need look no farther than this to find the prime precedent for Whitman's enormous catalogues: it is the essence of the prophet to comprehend the whole of the living earth within his view. But if Whitman is in this way a kind of prophet, for whom does he prophesy, for whom does he speak? "I celebrate myself, and sing myself," he declares in the opening bravado of his major poem. But what is this self? It is a something made up of "the thoughts of all men in all ages"; it is like "the grass that grows wherever the land is and the water is"; its "intricate purpose" is one with that of the "Fourth-month showers" and the "mica on the side of a rock." It is a universal sympathy, a universal consciousness, absorbing all into itself, becoming one with all and all with one:

Through me many long dumb voices,
Voices of the interminable generations of prisoners and slaves,
Voices of the diseas'd and despairing and of thieves and dwarfs . . .

When he listens he hears "all sounds running together, combined, fused or following"; when he touches he has "instant conductors all over me whether I pass or stop, / They seize every object and lead it harmlessly through me." As he says, smiling at the extravagance, nothing, nothing can evade him:

In vain the mastodon retreats beneath its own powder'd bones,
In vain objects stand leagues off and assume manifold shapes,
In vain the ocean settling in hollows and the great monsters lying low,

In vain the buzzard houses herself with the sky,
In vain the snake slides through the creepers and logs,
In vain the elk takes to the inner passes of the woods,
In vain the razor-bill'd auk sails far north to Labrador,
I follow quickly, I ascend to the nest in the fissure of the cliff.

Whatever happens, wherever it happens, "I am the man, I suffer'd, I was there."

Thus, in his vast prophetic catalogues we find each animal, each man and woman, caught in a characteristic occupation, vividly caught, and skillfully arranged in a list that is far more than a random listing. For his aim, as he says in "Proto-Leaf," 1860, is this:

. . . I will show that there is no imperfection in male or female, or in the earth, or in the present—and can be none in the future,
And I will show that whatever happens to anybody, it may be turned to beautiful results—And I will show that nothing can happen more beautiful than death;
And I will thread a thread through my poems that no one thing in the universe is inferior to another thing,
And that all the things of the universe are perfect miracles, each as profound as any.[3]

Hence, with a mild, leveling wit, we find Whitman placing the "elegant" and the "common," the "important" and the "trivial" side by side, with the bland assumption that all are of equal interest, equal value, whether it be the art-song of the trained singer or the art-sound of the carpenter's tool:

The pure contralto sings in the organ loft,
The carpenter dresses his plank, the tongue of his foreplane whistles its wild ascending lisp . . .
The duck-shooter walks by silent and cautious stretches,
The deacons are ordain'd with cross'd hands at the altar,

[3] See *Leaves of Grass: Facsimile Edition of the 1860 Text*, with introduction by Roy Harvey Pearce (Ithaca, N.Y., Cornell University Press, 1961).

The spinning-girl retreats and advances to the hum of the big
wheel,
The farmer stops by the bars as he walks on a First-day loafe and
looks at the oats and rye,
The lunatic is carried at last to the asylum a confirm'd case,
(He will never sleep any more as he did in the cot in his mother's
bed-room;)

Deacon and duck-shooter are equally reverent in their pursuits; spinning-girl and farmer have equally creative tasks; and even the madman has someone—his mother—for whom he has been an object of love and care.

The President holding a cabinet council is surrounded by the great
Secretaries,
On the piazza walk three matrons stately and friendly with twined
arms,
The crew of the fish-smack pack repeated layers of halibut in the
hold . . .

Cabinet council, twined matrons, packed layers of halibut thus come together in a thoroughly democratic equivalence!

The self he sings is nothing less than the power of his human consciousness: a divine power, enabling the prophet to "hear and behold God in every object," enabling him to say: "I find letters from God dropt in the street, and every one is sign'd by God's name." Yet it is also a power resident, in some measure, in every man: "It is you talking just as much as myself, I act as the tongue of you,/Tied in your mouth, in mine it begins to be loosen'd." "The mere fact consciousness," says Whitman, is an awesome miracle:

these forms, the power of motion,
The least insect or animal, the senses, eyesight, love,
The first step I say awed me and pleas'd me so much,
I have hardly gone and hardly wish'd to go any farther,
But stop and loiter all the time to sing it in ecstatic songs.

Verbal consciousness, fully developed, is enough, says Whitman, to assure us of our divinity. It is a fact that he apprehends, in his own favorite terms, by leaning, and loafing, and loitering, not by cogitation, not by analytic thinking. Consciousness, for Whitman, arises by accepting and encouraging to the full the miracles of "seeing, hearing, feeling." The universe for Whitman requires no rational explanation, no analysis, no theology: it is enough to be "the caresser of life wherever moving."

Moving, to live consciously in the full flow of the divine, creative process—this is the heart of Whitman's prophecy. Yet he is not a callow, easy optimist: he knows the hounded slave, the massacre in Texas, the "hiss of the surgeon's knife." Whitman is aware that the honest caresser of life must draw his fingers across the jagged points and the gaping wounds; and in his later poems he becomes ever more deeply aware of death, as in the conclusion of "Out of the Cradle Endlessly Rocking." But the sense of death, the melancholy moments, the awareness of the "down-hearted doubters"—all these things are absorbed into and transcended by the outgoing and onsweeping wonder of consciousness, brought to the peak of creativity by the wonder of the human word. "The words of the true poems give you more than poems," he declares:

Whom they take they take into space to behold the birth of stars, to learn one of the meanings,
To launch off with absolute faith, to sweep through the ceaseless rings and never be quiet again.

II

But Whitman's kind of poetry is not by any means for everyone, as Emily Dickinson may be taken to imply in a stringent little poem:

"Faith" is a fine invention
When Gentlemen can *see*—
But *Microscopes* are prudent
In an Emergency.

We do not know whether Emily ever read Whitman; certainly she had not in her earlier years, when she wrote to Higginson: "You speak of Mr. Whitman—I never read his Book—but was told that he was disgraceful." [4] There is probably a tongue-in-cheek tone here, for Emily would never have been shocked by his materials. She was not ashamed of "freckled human nature," as she called it. Indeed, to the conventional minds of her day, nothing in Whitman could be more shocking and disgraceful than her views in these desperate stanzas:

> The Heart asks Pleasure—first—
> And then—Excuse from Pain—
> And then—those little Anodynes
> That deaden suffering—
>
> And then—to go to sleep—
> And then—if it should be
> The will of it's Inquisitor
> The privilege to die—

Faith is a fine invention, as she says, for those who have it: let them be the seers, the prophets; let them be the caressers of life. But what shall be done for those who live in doubt, in fear, in danger, in anguish, in a state of emergency? For such as these, she says, the microscopic eye will serve better than the prophetic eye; those in doubt need to examine themselves in sharp detail, in order to find a cure and build a basis for living. Thus the poet of Emily Dickinson's kind cultivates the habit of self-analysis, sinks within the self to study all experience in close detail:

> I measure every Grief I meet
> With narrow, probing, Eyes—
> I wonder if It weighs like Mine—
> Or has an Easier size.

[4] *The Letters of Emily Dickinson*, ed. Thomas H. Johnson and Theodora Ward (3 vols., Cambridge, Harvard University Press, 1958), II, 404.

That is, with "analytic eyes," as Emily says in a variant reading of the second line. For the problem facing this poet is the stern task of recovering stability after some disastrous, shattering experience; the process is one of reconstructing the very self:

I felt a Cleaving in my Mind—
As if my Brain had split—
I tried to match it—Seam by Seam—
But could not make them fit.

The thought behind, I strove to join
Unto the thought before—
But Sequence ravelled out of Sound
Like Balls—upon a Floor.

The poem perfectly describes the essential exercise and aim of her poetry: to join thoughts deliberately, precisely, seam by seam, until a single condition of mind, a single experience, is full grasped, fully understood. Thus we have her deliberate, tough, unsparing analysis of the state of grief:

The last Night that She lived
It was a Common Night
Except the Dying—this to Us
Made Nature different

We noticed smallest things—
Things overlooked before
By this great light upon our Minds
Italicized—as 'twere.

* * * * *

We waited while She passed—
It was a narrow time—
Too jostled were Our Souls to speak
At length the notice came.

She mentioned, and forgot—
Then lightly as a Reed

Bent to the Water, struggled scarce—
Consented, and was dead—

And We—We placed the Hair—
And drew the Head erect—
And then an awful leisure was
Belief to regulate—

"Our faith to—regulate—" says Emily in another reading of the final line. It is a poem of emergency, microscopically developed, with every nuance of emotion understood—including the final immense difficulty of maintaining faith under such a blow. The word *regulate* is exactly right (a word that Whitman would have detested). All her poems show a lifetime's effort to *regulate* an individual existence, with all the rich meanings of that word: to put in good order, to adjust so as to work accurately, to dispose, arrange, direct, rule, govern, control.

Hence the technique of her verse becomes utterly opposite from Whitman's. The expression of her self-control, her self-understanding, must take these tersely measured forms, holding under tense command a dangerous charge. And in this self-command every microscopic detail of her verse plays a significant part: all the minutiae of spelling, line-arrangement, off-rhyme, and punctuation, which at last we now have accurately available in the new standard edition of her poetry.[5] The subtlety, the precision, of technique in her best poems may be seen with particular clarity when we compare these authentic texts with the altered versions produced by her earlier editors. Perhaps the best way to show this would be to concentrate upon the following famous poem as it now appears in the new edition:

[5] *The Poems of Emily Dickinson*, ed. Thomas H. Johnson (3 vols., Cambridge, Harvard University Press, 1955). Mr. Johnson's admirable annotation, especially his listing of textual variants, provides the basis for the following analysis of comparative readings. My quotations from Emily Dickinson's poetry are of course taken from this edition.

Because I could not stop for Death—
He kindly stopped for me—
The Carriage held but just Ourselves—
And Immortality.

We slowly drove—He knew no haste
And I had put away
My labor and my leisure too,
For His Civility—

We passed the school, where children strove
At Recess—in the Ring—
We passed the Fields of Gazing Grain—
We passed the Setting Sun—

Or rather—He passed Us—
The Dews drew quivering and chill—
For only Gossamer, my Gown—
My Tippet—only Tulle—

We paused before a House that seemed
A Swelling of the Ground—
The Roof was scarcely visible—
The Cornice—in the Ground—

Since then—'tis Centuries—and yet
Feels shorter than the Day
I first surmised the Horses Heads
Were toward Eternity—

A thoughtful reading of this text aloud will show how effectively the dashes indicate dramatic pause and pacing, and how accurately the capitals guide us toward a proper emphasis, as in the last stanza, where the "Centuries" are made to stand out in sharp contrast with the "Day," which then leads into the unbroken concluding speed-up toward the crashing word "Eternity." All this was lost in the old published version, where only two capitals were retained, and the frequent use of semicolons and periods (nine times) broke up the continuous dramatic action of the language. Moreover, we realize with something of a start, a whole stanza, the fourth, has been hitherto omitted and unknown; but now it seems impossible to do without it, for the strongly emphasized reversal ("—He passed Us—") indicates a sudden awakening to the passage of time: it is growing late, turning cold, and the speaker is caught unprepared, defenseless in her finery, while the word "Gossamer" seems to carry an eerie foreshadowing of the spider's web. One should note too that the details of this recovered stanza clearly characterize the speaker as a woman: an important fact in the atmosphere of ironic politeness and near-courtship that pervades the poem. At the same time the shock of realization is enforced here by a change in stanza-form; whereas the other stanzas beat forth the steady 4-3-4-3 of the ballad-form, this stanza of reversal shifts the footing to 3-4-4-3—an upsetting effect that perhaps motivated the omission by the early editors. Other alterations served to moderate the original pungent phrasing. In the third stanza "strove" was changed to "played," on the assumption, I suppose, that children should not "strive" at "recess"; but Emily's paradox is clear and sharp: play is stern competition to the child. At the same time the second line of this third stanza was changed to read: "Their lessons scarcely done," thus forming a proper rhyme with "sun." In the fifth stanza we had another "improvement": "The cornice but a mound"; this avoided the unseemly but accurate and insistent repetition of "Ground," and destroyed the understated impact of the original image, with its eerie architectural detail. And finally, the early editors conventionalized the syntax of the last stanza, giving "but each" in the first line for "and yet"; "each" thus refers neatly to "Centuries," but the original elliptical phrasing says much more—it says that all the time "since then" feels shorter than the day this speaker made her notable surmise.

Usually the alterations made within a single poem are not so extensive as those we have just seen: most of them consist of a word here, a word there, to set a rhyme, remove a localism, or normalize a peculiar usage—such as the author's addiction to the use of verbs in what may look like a subjunctive or hortatory way, when the indicative would normally be expected. This often amounts to a sort of elliptical condition (equal to "may be," "could be"); but perhaps it is best described as a way of achieving an effect of absolute, immediate action:

> Unmoved—she notes the Chariots—pausing—
> At her low Gate
> Unmoved—an Emperor be kneeling
> Upon her Mat—

The "be" was changed to "is" by the early editors.

Even where the changes within a given poem are very few, these often occur in a crucial position. Thus in the well-known poem of twelve stanzas, "I cannot live with You," we find only three words altered: but two of these occur in the last stanza, and change the meaning so drastically that the whole poem loses force. Here is the correct reading:

> So We must meet apart—
> You there—I—here—
> With just the Door ajar
> That Oceans are—and Prayer—
> And that White Sustenance—
> Despair—

In the old version "meet" was changed to "keep," thus spoiling the point of the poem: that these two must meet in this lover's agonized devotion, even though so distant in bodily fact. Then in the fifth line "White" was changed to "pale," thus destroying the ironical suggestion of the Manna. Or consider the small Herbertian poem, "Poor little Heart!" which concludes:

> Gay little Heart—
> Like Morning Glory!
> Wind and Sun—wilt thee array!

The last line was altered to read: "Thou'll wilted be; thou'll wilted be!" One ought also to note the opening stanza of this famous poem:

> There's a certain Slant of light,
> Winter Afternoons—
> That oppresses, like the Heft
> Of Cathedral Tunes—

The early editors added a small word in the second line, to read: "On winter afternoons," while "Heft" was changed to "weight" —and the effect of colloquial intimacy is lost. In poems as finely wrought as Emily Dickinson's best, the change of the slightest word may be enough to mar the working of the whole delicate organism.

Finally, consider the unique and subtle effects created by the dashes, capitals, quotation marks, and exclamation point in this brief poem:

> I shall know why—when Time is over—
> And I have ceased to wonder why—
> Christ will explain each separate anguish
> In the fair schoolroom of the sky—
>
> He will tell me what "Peter" promised—
> And I—for wonder at his woe—
> I shall forget the drop of Anguish
> That scalds me now—that scalds me now!

The old version, with all these pointings and pacings and emphases removed, is comparatively tame. The full bitterness of the ambiguous attitude does not emerge: we lose the easy ironical movement between lines two and three; we lose the doubt cast on "Peter's" identity; we lose the sense of inadequacy that this promise creates when set against "the drop of Anguish" that could produce the cry of the final line.

All these peculiar things, then, her localisms, her strangely effective use of the subjunctive form, her dashes and capitals, her willingness to vary stanza-form in the interest of a special emphasis, her love of half-rhyme, with its effect of informality, wryness, and surprise—all these things play their part in bringing us close to that inner meditative being which knows so well the "Hound within the Heart." It is an inner being poised on a hard-won point, from which the meditative vision reaches out to see "Eternity's vast pocket, picked," to find that Gethsemane "Is but a Province—in the Being's Centre." From that center, gained and maintained by rigorous self-analysis, she can assail "These Gentlewomen" of "Dimity Convictions," who show

> A Horror so refined
> Of freckled Human Nature—
> Of Deity—ashamed—

For her Deity, like George Herbert's, is one who never minds an honest disagreement or a "freckled" opinion. She can take issue with his justice and sympathize with "that Old Moses" who, like herself, was barred from the promised land; somehow, she feels, the "Romance" of Moses "In point of injury" surpasses that "Of Stephen—or of Paul—"

> For these—were only put to death—
> While God's adroiter will
>
> On Moses—seemed to fasten
> With tantalizing Play
> As Boy—should deal with lesser Boy—
> To prove ability.

She can subtly mock the Calvinistic vision of a God whose arbitrary will violates her passionate belief in the value of each individual being:

> It's easy to invent a Life—
> God does it—every Day—
> Creation—but the Gambol
> Of His Authority—

It's easy to efface it—
The thrifty Deity
Could scarce afford Eternity
To Spontaneity—

The Perished Patterns murmur—
But His Perturbless Plan
Proceed—inserting Here—a Sun—
There—leaving out a Man—

Such a theology, though perhaps entertained as a possibility in moments of bitterness, is ultimately not to be endured by one who could write:

To be alive—is Power—
Existence—in itself—
Without a further function—
Omnipotence—Enough—

To be alive—and Will!
'Tis able as a God—
The Maker—of Ourselves—be what—
Such being Finitude!

That inner confidence in the validity of the creative Will enables her to maintain "This Consciousness that is aware / Of Neighbors and the Sun," to hold her Deity and her pet dog within a single purview, to address God as though she were addressing a note to her sister-in-law Sue or to some other friend. I think we can see this in a remarkable poem which the new edition prints from a copy signed (like many of her poems) "Emily"; this copy, the editor says, "was sent to an unidentified recipient." [6] But the ultimate recipient seems to be divine: the allusion to a "dizzy knee" suggests the superhuman:

What shall I do—it whimpers so—
This little Hound within the Heart
All day and night with bark and start—

[6] *Poems of Emily Dickinson*, ed. Johnson, I, 135.

And yet, it will not go—
Would you *untie* it, were you me—
Would it stop whining—if to Thee—
I sent it—even now?

It should not tease you—
By your chair—or, on the mat—
Or if it dare—to climb your dizzy knee—
Or—sometimes at your side to run—
When you were willing—
Shall it come?
Tell Carlo—
He'll tell *me!*

This suggestion of a double address is found in a number of her best poems, especially in her love-poems, where she sometimes writes in a way akin (though ultimately opposite) to Herbert's mode of adapting the idiom of popular love-poetry in appeals to his divine Friend. This poem strikes a clear Herbertian note:

That I did always love
I bring thee Proof
That till I loved
I never lived—Enough—

That I shall love alway—
I argue thee
That love is life—
And life hath Immortality—

This—dost thou doubt—Sweet—
Then have I
Nothing to show
But Calvary—

Taken by itself, the poem could be addressed either to Christ or to a human lover; in the context of her other poems it emerges as a guarded address to her human love; as in good Petrarchan poetry, the religious element serves to exalt earthly love. She is turning Herbert's technique back to the service from which he had attempted to divert it.

In other poems of this sort the balance is hardly in doubt, as in the famous "Wild Nights," which gave some pause to Higginson in choosing poems for the 1891 edition: "One poem only," wrote Higginson, "I dread a little to print—that wonderful 'Wild Nights,'—lest the malignant read into it more than that virgin recluse ever dreamed of putting there. Has Miss Lavinia any shrinking about it? You will understand & pardon my solicitude. Yet what a loss to omit it! Indeed it is not to be omitted." [7] The slight ambiguity of the wording could allow Higginson to take a spiritual view of its meaning; yet the poem seems essentially sexual. One poem, above all, can leave us in no doubt about the physical nature of her passion; in "I cannot live with You" she sets her two lords face to face, declaring:

> Nor could I rise—with You—
> Because Your Face
> Would put out Jesus'—
> That New Grace
>
> Glow plain—and foreign
> On my homesick Eye—
> Except that You than He
> Shone closer by—
>
> They'd judge Us—How—
> For you—served Heaven—You know,
> Or sought to—
> I could not—
>
> Because You saturated Sight—

No wonder, then, that when Higginson said the "gait" of her poems was "spasmodic," she gave the terse, polite rebuke: "I am in danger—Sir." [8]

But these unhappy moods are only one aspect of her mani-

[7] *Poems of Emily Dickinson*, ed. Johnson, I, 180.
[8] *Letters of Emily Dickinson*, ed. Johnson and Ward, II, 409.

fold interior existence; there are many other experiences for her to analyse: the humorous, half-mocking interpretation of what it must feel like to be a locomotive, in "I like to see it lap the Miles," where she treats the engine as though it really were an iron horse; or the gaiety of certain moods in summer and spring:

Inebriate of Air—am I—
And Debauchee of Dew—
Reeling—thro endless summer days—
From inns of Molten Blue—

When "Landlords" turn the drunken Bee
Out of the Foxglove's door—
When Butterflies—renounce their "drams"—
I shall but drink the more!

Or we have Emily's amused and affectionate treatment of a small child, not very clean, to whom she has evidently given a bun—and won his thanks:

This dirty—little—Heart
Is freely mine.
I won it with a Bun—
A Freckled shrine—

But eligibly fair
To him who sees
The Visage of the Soul
And not the knees.

That poem will serve to remind us of the domestic, local quality of Emily Dickinson's poetry: she does not point out to us the Promised Land from the top of a mountain, as Whitman does. She raises her eternal questions in the midst of a small locale of neighbors, dogs, boys, flowers, doors, balls of knitting yarn, buttons, bumble-bees, brooches, spectacles, latches, shelves for silver and china, buckets, sleds, streets, and church steeples. It is more than appropriate, then, that hundreds of Emily's poems should have come down to us, as Mrs. Bingham describes them, "written on the backs of brown-paper bags or of discarded bills, programs, and invitations; on tiny scraps of stationery pinned together; on leaves torn from old notebooks . . . on soiled and mildewed subscription blanks, or on department- or drug-store bargain flyers from Amherst and surrounding towns. There are pink scraps, blue and yellow scraps, one of them a wrapper of *Chocolat Meunier*; poems on the reverse of recipes in her own writing, on household shopping lists, on the cut-off margins of newspapers." One poem resides complete on the back of a printed slip that reads:

> This Lamp, bearing upon the Chimney Gallery and upon the Thumbscrew, the name of *The German Student Lamp Co.*, is hereby guaranteed to be perfect in all its parts, to burn properly and not to leak.[9]

We can guarantee the same of her best poetry.

Her genius lives within this domestic atmosphere; her discoveries are made "in the Being's Centre," as in this poem where she comes as close to Whitman as she will ever come:

> The Brain—is wider than the Sky—
> For—put them side by side—
> The one the other will contain
> With ease—and You—beside—
>
> The Brain is deeper than the sea—
> For—hold them—Blue to Blue—
> The one the other will absorb—
> As Sponges—Buckets—do—
>
> The Brain is just the weight of God—
> For—Heft them—Pound for Pound—
> And they will differ—if they do—
> As Syllable from Sound—

[9] *Bolts of Melody: New Poems of Emily Dickinson*, ed. Mabel Loomis Todd and Millicent Todd Bingham (New York, Harper & Brothers, 1945), pp. xii-xv.

Heft was changed to *lift* in the old editions, but the colloquial, country word brings God home to the mind in a peculiarly intimate and local way. It is the kind of syllable by which the brain of the meditative poet gives voice to the mysterious sound of God's presence.

It is important to note the difference in the association between brain and sky, brain and sea, or brain and God, when we compare this poem with Whitman's "Song of Myself." Whitman's way of absorbing all things into his consciousness results finally in the dispersal of the self throughout the universe:

> I depart as air, I shake my white locks at the runaway sun,
> I effuse my flesh in eddies, and drift it in lacy jags.
>
> I bequeath myself to the dirt to grow from the grass I love,
> If you want me again look for me under your boot-soles.

In Whitman the prophetic voice moves from the individual into the cosmos, and in the end we have too often a voice without a body, fading into the Abstract and the Absolute. But this is not for Emily: in every mood and crisis the individual brain struggles to maintain its ultimate control, its unremitting, individual grip on the microscopic details of human existence:

> I heard a Fly buzz—when I died—
> The Stillness in the Room
> Was like the Stillness in the Air—
> Between the Heaves of Storm—

So, out of her reading in the English poets of the seventeenth century, out of her familiarity with old hymns, out of her heritage of Puritan introspection, out of the Emersonian view of nature, and out of her incalculable genius, she created the self that lives within her meditative poetry:

> What fortitude the Soul contains,
> That it can so endure
> The accent of a coming Foot—
> The opening of a Door—

VI

T. S. Eliot:
The Wheel and the Point

MARIANNE MOORE once acutely remarked that Eliot's poems "are so consistently intricated that one rests on another and is involved with what was earlier." Thus *Four Quartets* rests firmly on a basis of imagery and theme built up by Eliot's other works; and this may be said of all his poems: any given one is best apprehended in the context provided by the body of Eliot's achievement. This is true of all poets in some degree; indeed, assessing the degree of "intrication" among a poet's various works may be one element in deciding the problem of greatness. With these concerns in mind, I should like to explore Eliot's symbol of "the still point," the dominant symbol of his poetry since *The Waste Land,* and at the same time to stress the significance of *Murder in the Cathedral.*

The relation of this play to the core of Eliot's poetry is shown in Becket's first words, addressed to the priest who has been rebuking the Chorus for its lamentations:

> Peace. And let them be, in their exaltation.
> They speak better than they know, and beyond your under-
> standing.
> They know and do not know, what it is to act or suffer.
> They know and do not know, that acting is suffering
> And suffering is action. Neither does the actor suffer
> Nor the patient act. But both are fixed

In an eternal action, an eternal patience
To which all must consent that it may be willed
And which all must suffer that they may will it,
That the pattern may subsist, for the pattern is the action
And the suffering, that the wheel may turn and still
Be forever still.

A pattern of double meaning resides in the words, *suffering, patient,* and *patience. Suffering* is not simply *undergoing misery* or *pain;* it is also *permitting, consenting;* he who consents to an action must suffer for it, must accept responsibility for it. The Chorus of Women of Canterbury, the "type of the common man," understands no such responsibility as the play begins: "For us, the poor, there is no action,/But only to wait and to witness." It is this responsibility that the women strive to evade as they realize they are being "drawn into the pattern of fate"; this is what they finally admit at their great moment of exaltation and vision: "I have consented, Lord Archbishop, have consented." It is the admission of sin which Eliot describes and demands in his prose writings—in the essay on Baudelaire's *Journaux Intimes,* for example, where he insists that "the recognition of the reality of Sin is a New Life," and finds the greatness of Baudelaire (like the greatness of the Chorus here) to reside in his capacity for suffering pain in the knowledge of good which comes from the knowledge of evil. It is the view expressed in one of Eliot's notes to *The Idea of a Christian Society:* "The notion of communal responsibility, of the responsibility of every individual for the sins of the society to which he belongs, is one that needs to be more firmly apprehended."

Thus, too, the *patient* is everyone, martyr, murderer, and spectator: he is at once suffering pain and permitting action; in Becket and the Chorus, he is also self-controlled. The same ideas are seen in the lyric of "East Coker," where the "hospital" patient is saved by Christ from "Adam's curse": "Beneath the bleeding hands we feel/The sharp compassion of the healer's art." Becket is the Christ of his age, who by suffering heals those who also suffer, as he explains just before his martyrdom:

We are not here to triumph by fighting, by stratagem, or by resistance,
Not to fight with beasts as men. We have fought the beast
And have conquered. We have only to conquer
Now, by suffering. This is the easier victory.
Now is the triumph of the Cross, now
Open the door!

This eternally decreed pattern of suffering, which is also action, and of action, which is also suffering, Eliot symbolizes by the image of the wheel which always turns, yet, at the axis, always remains still. This image lies at the heart of Eliot's poetry. In *Ash Wednesday:*

> Against the Word the unstilled world still whirled
> About the centre of the silent Word.

In the two *Coriolan* poems:

> O hidden under the dove's wing, hidden in the turtle's breast,
> Under the palmtree at noon, under the running water
> At the still point of the turning world. O hidden.

Above all, in the two fragments from Heraclitus which preface "Burnt Norton" and announce the theme of all the *Four Quartets.* The first fragment is closely related to the above passage from *Ash Wednesday:* "But though the Word is common [*central,* in Eliot's image], the many live as though they had a wisdom of their own." The wheel image is more clearly suggested in the second fragment, which is best read with the fragment (LXX) and editorial note immediately following in the Loeb Library edition, for the words of Fragment LXX echo throughout the *Four Quartets:*

LXIX. The road up and the road down is one and the same.
LXX. The beginning and end are common.

Heraclitus is referring to a point on the circumference of a circle.

These fragments appear in "The Dry Salvages": "And the way up is the way down, the way forward is the way back"; but the image of the wheel is presented most extensively in Section II of "Burnt Norton," opening with the image of "the bedded axle-tree," and continuing with the familiar words:

At the still point of the turning world. Neither flesh nor fleshless;
Neither from nor towards; at the still point, there the dance is,
But neither arrest nor movement.

Here is *Peace*—Becket's first word in the play—the end which all patients and actors in the play, guided or misguided, seek after in their various ways: the Knights by violent worldly action; the Priests by flight and barricade; the Chorus by an attempt to remain unconscious, inactive, seeking a "peace" which is only the refuge of animals: "And the labourer bends to his piece of earth, earth-colour, his own colour,/Preferring to pass unobserved"; Becket alone by the true path of conscious submission to the central Word, as explained by his definition of *Peace* in the Christmas sermon. Becket's death is thus the still point of the world that turns within the play.

This is the theme which unifies Eliot's poetry from the words of Buddha and St. Augustine in *The Waste Land* to "the unimaginable zero summer," the still point symbolized by the ascetic ritual of Little Gidding. Becket and the religious community of Nicholas Ferrar have for Eliot much the same symbolic meaning—a meaning also found by Eliot in Pascal and the religious community of Port-Royal. Indeed, the implication of the whole body of Eliot's writing is nowhere better illustrated than in the interrelation between *Murder in the Cathedral*, "Little Gidding," and Eliot's essay on the *Pensées* of Pascal. Becket, Ferrar, and Pascal are, as this essay suggests, symbols of "one kind of religious believer, which is highly passionate and ardent, but passionate only through a powerful and regulated intellect . . . facing unflinchingly the demon of doubt which is inseparable from the spirit of belief." Of all three it might be said that "he had the knowledge of worldliness and the passion of asceticism, and in him the two are fused into an individual whole." All are symbols to be recommended "to those who doubt, but who have the mind to conceive, and the sensibility to feel, the disorder, the futility, the meaninglessness, the mystery of life and suffering, and who can only find peace through a satisfaction of the whole being."

This still point of peace is variously symbolized throughout Eliot's poetry, and the variety of the symbols may obscure the connection between Eliot's image of the "rose-garden" and Becket. The "rose-garden," as Mr. Unger explains in his study of this image,[1] represents in Eliot a moment of contact with reality, a moment of rare consciousness and "sudden illumination," which flashes across the drab flux of ordinary life as the only meaningful moment (or moments) of that life—an experience which the individual may try constantly and unsuccessfully to recapture. It is, in short, the "still point" in the life of the individual.

The image of the rose-garden is used most clearly in *Ash Wednesday*, "Burnt Norton," and *The Family Reunion*, but with important differences of reference. In *Ash Wednesday* the rose is explicitly religious in significance, suggesting Dante's "rosa sempiterna" of Paradise. In "Burnt Norton" and *The Family Reunion* the image appears to draw part of its power and meaning from two other sources in literature which have not been generally noted. Mr. Eliot has remarked in conversation upon the importance of *Alice in Wonderland* here. As most readers

[1] Leonard Unger, "T. S. Eliot's Rose Garden: A Persistent Theme," *Southern Review*, 7 (1942), 667-89.

will recall, Alice, near the beginning of her adventures, is wandering about "in a long, low hall" where she finds a "golden key" that fits the lock of "a little door."

> Alice opened the door and found that it led into a small passage . . . she knelt down and looked along the passage into the loveliest garden you ever saw. How she longed to get out of that dark hall, and wander about among those beds of bright flowers and those cool fountains, but she could not even get her head through the doorway.

From then on, despite her adventures, Alice never forgets "the little door into that lovely garden"; "I've got back to my right size: the next thing is, to get into that beautiful garden—how *is* that to be done, I wonder?" It is not until well past the middle of her story that she finally walks "down the little passage: and *then*—she found herself at last in the beautiful garden, among the bright flower-beds and the cool fountains." True, it is not a rose-garden, but it does contain the famous white rose-tree, where the gardeners are busily painting the roses red.

In "Burnt Norton":

> Footfalls echo in the memory
> Down the passage which we did not take
> Towards the door we never opened
> Into the rose-garden. . . .
>
> Other echoes
> Inhabit the garden. Shall we follow?
> Quick, said the bird, find them, find them,
> Round the corner. Through the first gate,
> Into our first world, shall we follow
> The deception of the thrush? Into our first world.

The experience of Alice becomes in Eliot a symbol of the longing to be born again, a symbol of the search for spiritual refreshment, for a change of heart, a change of vision, as in this dream-scene of "Burnt Norton," where "the leaves were full of children,/Hidden excitedly, containing laughter." The Alice-imagery carries the same suggestions in *The Family Reunion:*

> You bring me news
> Of a door that opens at the end of a corridor,
> Sunlight and singing. . . .
>
> I only looked through the little door
> When the sun was shining on the rose-garden:
> And heard in the distance tiny voices. . . .
>
> And what did not happen is as true as what did happen,
> O my dear, and you walked through the little door
> And I ran to meet you in the rose-garden.

But other echoes inhabit this garden. The imagery of Alice seems to be merged with memories of another garden experience, related in D. H. Lawrence's story, "The Shadow in the Rose Garden" (in *The Prussian Officer*, 1914), which Eliot praises and discusses at some length in *After Strange Gods.* If one adds the traditional associations between human love and love of the divine, the experience of the woman in Lawrence's story is very close in symbolic meaning to Eliot's conception of the still point in "Burnt Norton":

> To be conscious is not to be in time
> But only in time can the moment in the rose-garden,
> The moment in the arbour where the rain beat,
> The moment in the draughty church at smokefall
> Be remembered; involved with past and future.
> Only through time time is conquered.

Lawrence's woman seeks to recapture the experience of an early love by revisiting the rose-garden where the experience had occurred, a garden in bright sunlight, with "blue sea" visible beyond:

> . . . she came to a high wall by the wayside. Under this she went slowly, stopping at length by an open doorway, which shone like a picture of light in the dark wall. There in the magic beyond the

doorway, patterns of shadow lay on the sunny court. . . . She tiptoed nervously into the courtyard. . . . Irresolutely she took a step forward, and again forward, leaning, yearning, towards the garden beyond. . . .

Slowly she went down one path, lingering, like one who has gone back into the past. Suddenly she was touching some heavy crimson roses that were soft as velvet, touching them thoughtfully, without knowing, as a mother sometimes fondles the hand of her child. . . . Then she wandered on in abstraction. Sometimes a flame-coloured, scentless rose would hold her arrested. She stood gazing at it as if she could not understand it. . . . So, slowly, like a white, pathetic butterfly, she drifted down the path, coming at last to a tiny terrace all full of roses. They seemed to fill the place, a sunny, gay throng. She was shy of them, they were so many and so bright. They seemed to be conversing and laughing. She felt herself in a strange crowd. It exhilarated her, carried her out of herself. . . .

Then she started cruelly as a shadow crossed her and a figure moved into her sight. It was a man who had come in slippers, unheard. He wore a linen coat. The morning was shattered, the spell vanished away.

It is her lover, whom she had thought dead, but who is now amazingly before her in the flesh—beyond redemption, as she realizes "with horror," for he is insane:

The woman turned and walked swiftly, blindly, between the sunny roses, out from the garden, past the house with the blank, dark windows, through the sea-pebbled courtyard to the street. Hastening and blind, she went forward without hesitating, not knowing whither.

The doorway, the sunlight, the water, the roses, the illusion of a crowd, the laughter, the shattered moment of illumination—all point inevitably toward "Burnt Norton" and *The Family Reunion:*

I only looked through the little door
When the sun was shining on the rose-garden:
And heard in the distance tiny voices

And then a black raven flew over.
And then I was only my own feet walking
Away, down a concrete corridor
In a dead air. Only feet walking
And sharp heels scraping.

I believe, too, that in Eliot's line, "The moment in the arbour where the rain beat," one finds added significance by recalling Joyce's story, "The Dead," which Eliot analyzes and praises, along with Lawrence's story, in *After Strange Gods*. In "The Dead" the significant moment is the wife's sudden vision of her long-dead lover, standing in the garden in heavy rain, "at the end of the wall where there was a tree."

At the same time these allusions to a door, to a garden, and to the laughter of children at a distance seem to have some relation to Eliot's own childhood. As he tells us in an attractive, little-known memoir,[2] his early years in St. Louis were spent in a house situated next to a girls' school that was closely associated with Eliot's family: "There was at the front of our house a sort of picket fence which divided our front yard from the schoolyard. This picket fence merged a little later as it passed the wall of the house into a high brick wall which concealed our back garden from the schoolyard and also concealed the schoolyard from our back garden. There was a door in this wall and there was a key to this door." Eliot tells how, after school hours, he used to make this schoolyard his own private playground and how sometimes he ventured into the school itself after everyone had left, and "wandered about the corridors." Of course, he adds, when the girls "were in the schoolyard I was always on the other side of the wall; and on one occasion I remember, when I ventured into the schoolyard a little too early when there were

[2] See the brief address given by Eliot in 1959 at the centennial celebration of Mary Institute, a girls' school in St. Louis founded by Eliot's grandfather, named for Eliot's Aunt Mary (who died at the age of 17), and attended by Eliot's sisters. The address is printed in the centennial issue of the school's publication, *From Mary to You*, pp. 133-6.

still a few on the premises and I saw them staring at me through a window, I took flight at once." One should note too that in this schoolyard, Eliot says, "I remember a mound on which stood a huge ailanthus tree. . . . And I have a photograph of myself standing against this ailanthus tree at the age of seven or eight in the company of a crony of the same age." No doubt this memory has some relation to the "rank ailanthus" mentioned in the opening of "The Dry Salvages." Thus personal memories of a "first world" appear to be intermingled with literary echoes and with the present scene at the English country house to create the unexpected moment of illumination with which "Burnt Norton" opens.

That moment may be an actual experience in the past, or an experience only desired, never achieved. But the desire for this still point where all desires end is the saving grace; the unredeemable or unconsummated moment in the worldly garden is related to and indeed leads on to the Rose of Paradise, for the object of desire is a moment of timeless reality, apprehended in the world of time. The whole rose-garden scene of "Burnt Norton" suggests the words of St. Bernard in Dante's Paradise: "That thou mayest consummate thy journey perfectly . . . fly with thine eyes throughout this garden; for gazing on it will equip thy glance better to mount through the divine ray" (Canto xxxi). The religious implications of this imagery are enhanced by the echoes of St. Augustine's *Confessions* which, I think, introduce and conclude the description of the rose-garden in "Burnt Norton." Recall Eliot's meditation here on the theme that "Time past and time future . . ./Point to one end, which is always present"; recall that "Footfalls echo in the memory," that "My words echo/Thus, in your mind," leading to the evocation of the imagery of the rose-garden as a memory of a possible childhood experience. Then read Augustine's section on the problem of time (*Confessions,* Book XI), especially this passage:

For if there be times past, and times to come; fain would I know where they be: which yet if I be not able to conceive, yet thus much I know, that wheresoever they now be, they are not there future or past, but present. For if there also, future they be, then are they not there yet: if there also they be past, then are they not there still. Wheresoever therefore and whatsoever they be, they are not but as present. Although as for things past, whenever true stories are related, out of the memory are drawn not the things themselves which are past, but such words as being conceived by the images of those things, they, in their passing through our senses, have, as their footsteps, left imprinted in our minds. For example, mine own childhood, which at this instant is not . . . but as for the image of it, when I call that to mind, and tell of it, I do even in the present behold it, because it is still in my memory. (Ch. XVIII, Loeb Library trans.)

Indeed, in this book of the *Confessions* (Ch. XI) Augustine expresses the central question of Eliot's later poetry:

Who will hold [the heart of man], and so fix it, that it may stand a while, and a little catch at a beam of light from that ever-fixed eternity, to compare it with the times which are never fixed, that he may thereby perceive how there is no comparison between them . . . and that all both past and to come, is made up, and flows out of that which is always present? Who now shall so hold fast this heart of man, that it may stand, and see, how that eternity ever still standing, gives the word of command to the times past or to come, itself being neither past nor to come? Can my hand do this, or can the hand of my mouth by speech, bring about so important a business?

The difficulty is that the search for the still point involves the grasping of so many false points—a confusion represented in the *Coriolan* poems, which are closely related to *Murder in the Cathedral*. In "Triumphal March" the crowd is seeking desperately for "light," for a still point in the meaningless flux of life without faith, where the Sanctus bell announces only "crumpets." As they watch the parade of death and daily banality, they find the supreme moment, mistakenly, in their glimpse of the worldly Leader. The terror of clinging to such a "point" is displayed in "Difficulties of a Statesman," where the Leader, lost in the flux of worldly affairs, is himself desperately searching for "a still moment, repose of noon." Becket's career, as presented in the play, provides the best commentary on *Coriolan*. The still point of peace for which all cry is not of this world, though it may be glimpsed in this world, as Becket's Christmas sermon shows: "He gave to His disciples peace, but not peace as the world gives."

To this theme of the timeless reality glimpsed in the world of time Eliot returns again and again in *Four Quartets*, with constant parallels to *Murder in the Cathedral*. Thus, in "The Dry Salvages":

> Men's curiosity searches past and future
> And clings to that dimension. But to apprehend
> The point of intersection of the timeless
> With time, is an occupation for the saint—
> No occupation either, but something given
> And taken, in a lifetime's death in love,
> Ardour and selflessness and self-surrender.
> For most of us, there is only the unattended
> Moment, the moment in and out of time,
> The distraction fit, lost in a shaft of sunlight. . . .

Among the saints who are thus prepared to recognize the moment when it comes are Augustine, Becket, Pascal, and the devotees of Little Gidding; the Chorus of the play represents "most of us," unable to anticipate, to understand, or to arrest the timeless moment.

The death of Becket, then, is one of these moments of illumination, equivalent to a moment in the rose-garden: a parallel enforced by Eliot's use of an identical sentence after the illumination in both "Burnt Norton" and *Murder in the Cathedral:* "Human kind cannot bear very much reality."

> Dry the pool, dry concrete, brown edged,
> And the pool was filled with water out of sunlight,
> And the lotos rose, quietly, quietly,

> The surface glittered out of heart of light,
> And they were behind us, reflected in the pool.
> Then a cloud passed, and the pool was empty.
> Go, said the bird, for the leaves were full of children,
> Hidden excitedly, containing laughter.
> Go, go, go, said the bird: human kind
> Cannot bear very much reality.

The experience is at once real and illusory. It is real because it represents one of those rare moments when humanity recognizes its deep need for contact with the "heart of light"—the still point, the Word, Dante's "deep light." As in any mirage, the sight of water signifies an intense feeling of need. The vision, however, is illusory, because it can only be experienced through the insubstantial forms of "time." For average humanity this effect of illusion is necessary, since such a moment of perception is too intense to be borne for long:

> the enchainment of past and future
> Woven in the weakness of the changing body,
> Protects mankind from heaven and damnation
> Which flesh cannot endure.

For the saint, however, such a perception is neither unbearable nor illusory, since he understands the true significance of the earthly moment and sees the higher realm in which the need will be satisfied. Hence Becket is able to explain the torment of the Chorus in its great cry, "I have smelt them, the death-bringers," which ends with the recognition of deep guilt and of deep need for a mediator:

> I have consented, Lord Archbishop, have consented.
> Am torn away, subdued, violated,
> United to the spiritual flesh of nature,
> Mastered by the animal powers of spirit,
> Dominated by the lust of self-demolition,
> By the final utter uttermost death of spirit,
> By the final ecstasy of waste and shame,
> O Lord Archbishop, O Thomas Archbishop, forgive us,

forgive us, pray for us that we may pray for you, out
of our shame.

The agony of the Women here, as the sexual imagery shows, comes from recognizing the degradation of humanity into the animal; and the echo of Shakespeare's "The expense of spirit in a waste of shame" extends the horror. In suffering their Lord to die, they feel "torn away" from the source of light. Becket's answer is very close to "Burnt Norton":

Peace, and be at peace with your thoughts and visions.
These things had to come to you and you to accept them.
This is your share of the eternal burden,
The perpetual glory. This is one moment,
But know that another
Shall pierce you with a sudden painful joy
When the figure of God's purpose is made complete.
You shall forget these things, toiling in the household,
You shall remember them, droning by the fire,
When age and forgetfulness sweeten memory
Only like a dream that has often been told
And often been changed in the telling. They will seem unreal.
Human kind cannot bear very much reality.

These passages in "Burnt Norton" and the play may seem far apart, since one relates to a vision of beauty and the other to a vision of ugliness. But the two visions lead to one end. Either is an escape from the world of Hollow Men, which, says Eliot in "Burnt Norton,"

. . . is a place of disaffection
Time before and time after
In a dim light: neither daylight
Investing form with lucid stillness
Turning shadow into transient beauty
With slow rotation suggesting permanence
Nor darkness to purify the soul
Emptying the sensual with deprivation
Cleansing affection from the temporal.

The "daylight" is equivalent to the moment in the rose-garden; the darkness is equivalent to that "Dark Night of the Soul" of St. John of the Cross, the religious purgation which has been well explained by Mr. Unger in relation to *Ash Wednesday* and "Burnt Norton," and by Mr. Sweeney in relation to "East Coker." [3] Both ways lead to reality and to salvation, though they appear to be moving in opposite directions ("the way up is the way down"). The way of the Dark Night leads down through a stage of utter disgust with the physical (as in the above chorus) and reaches at the bottom a state of vacancy, where sense and spirit alike are momentarily nullified—a low point from which one can only return upward to grace. It is this state which the Chorus describes in its final chant as "the loneliness of the night of God, the surrender required, the deprivation inflicted."

One may clarify the interrelation of these symbols by dividing them into three channels to reality. The average man has two approaches. The first is through the physical and sensuous: through the rose-garden and its related symbols of natural beauty, freshness, and fertility: the hyacinth girl, childish laughter, the bird's song. The second is the opposite way of the Dark Night. The third way, reserved for superior individuals, leads directly upward, "Light upon light, mounting the saint's stair," as Eliot says in "A Song for Simeon."

Hence Becket and the Chorus simultaneously achieve stillness at opposite poles: Becket in a vision of ultimate being, the Chorus in a vision of ultimate nullity:

Becket: I have had a tremor of bliss, a wink of heaven, a whisper,
And I would no longer be denied; all things
Proceed to a joyful consummation.

Chorus: Emptiness, absence, separation from God;
The horror of the effortless journey, to the empty land

[3] Leonard Unger, "Notes on *Ash Wednesday*," *Southern Review*, 4 (1939), 745-70; and the essay cited in footnote 1. James Johnson Sweeney, "East Coker: A Reading," *Southern Review*, 6 (1941), 771-91.

> Which is no land, only emptiness, absence, the Void,
> Where those who were men can no longer turn the mind
> To distraction, delusion, escape into dream, pretence,
> Where the soul is no longer deceived, for there are no objects, no tones,
> No colours, no forms to distract, to divert the soul
> From seeing itself, foully united forever, nothing with nothing. . . .

This experience of purgation is similar to that of *Ash Wednesday*. The Chorus is detached from the world to face a moment of reality, and the vision of utter destruction which it sees is really the road to exaltation. The passage just cited is the lowest point of the Chorus, although horror reaches greater intensity in the next chant, during the murder of Becket. In the latter the Women are really on the upward way, but, as usual, they misunderstand, "They know and do not know":

> Clear the air! clean the sky! wash the wind! take stone from stone and wash them.
> The land is foul, the water is foul, our beasts and ourselves defiled with blood.
> A rain of blood has blinded my eyes. Where is England? where is Kent? where is Canterbury?
> O far far far far in the past: and I wander in a land of barren boughs: if I break them, they bleed; I wander in a land of dry stones: if I touch them, they bleed.

The blood of Becket is purification, not defilement, for those who are contrite and ask for cleansing. The rain of blood is akin to Eliot's usual symbol of redemption, the water for which the Waste Land cries. And in this passage, together with suggestions of an Egyptian plague, of the land of Polydorus, of the stones leading to Dante's river of Blood, and of the bleeding boughs of the Suicides in the *Inferno* (Cantos xii and xiii), we have a specific echo of Eliot's own *Waste Land:* "And the dead tree gives no shelter, the cricket no relief,/And the dry stone no sound of water."

The Chorus, in fact, has begun the play in exactly the state described in the opening lines of *The Waste Land:* the state of those who fear a conscious life:

> Now I fear disturbance of the quiet seasons:
> Winter shall come bringing death from the sea,
> Ruinous spring shall beat at our doors,
> Root and shoot shall eat our eyes and our ears,
> Disastrous summer burn up the beds of our streams
> And the poor shall wait for another decaying October.

As in "Burnt Norton," these things are seen "in a shaft of sunlight," though the Chorus would avoid the illumination, "living and partly living"—living, that is, an animal existence, not the full life of conscious humanity. Salvation comes through the gradual growth of consciousness and the acknowledgment of sin.

The choruses of the play thus echo and prophesy the whole development of Eliot's poetry. The chorus opening Part II, which was substituted in the second edition of the play for the ecclesiastical procession of the original version, is closely related to the garden scene of "Burnt Norton," to "A Song for Simeon," to "Marina," to the *Landscapes,* "New Hampshire," "Rannoch," and "Cape Ann," and, in its imagery of the bird's song amid barrenness, to the many other places where Eliot uses this imagery of desired fertility and rebirth. This revision seems to me an improvement over the original Biblical chants, partly because it strengthens the play's unity by showing the effect of Becket's sermon on the Chorus, which here no longer fears the coming of Spring; and also because the revision is closer to the heart of Eliot's poetry and thus draws strength, as do the other choruses, from connection with the body of the poet's work.

To illustrate these relations fully, I should like to concentrate upon the difficult chorus already cited, that of "the deathbringers." Readers have disagreed widely in the evaluation of this, some placing it among "the greatest poetry of our day," others declaring that its "force is just violence, not really poetic force." Misunderstanding and dissatisfaction arise from viewing this chorus as simply "a prescience of evil"; it is certainly this, but not simply this. Eliot is creating here the vision of a universe without order, a vision given in the only way in which the "type of the common man" can realize it, by all the "quickened senses." The order of time is abolished: the merry fluting of a summer afternoon is heard at night mingled with the owl's "hollow note of death." Bats, with the huge scaly wings of Lucifer, slant over the noon sky. The creative mind of God and Man is gone; the scavengers and the least sensitive, least conscious forms of life take over. The threat of death exists even in the most delicate flowers. And with this disorder humanity feels its involvement: "I have lain on the floor of the sea and breathed with the breathing of the sea-anemone, swallowed with ingurgitation of the sponge." But, paradoxically, the Women are saved, not lost, by such a vision, for here gradually emerges the human consciousness at highest intensity, recognizing all creation as part of a pattern which points to this moment, seeing themselves as "death-bringers," admitting sin, crying for absolution. The disorder in the first two-thirds of this chorus, with its long, irresolute lines, changes to a balanced order of versification, phrasing, and thought as the Chorus recognizes its responsibility:

> Have I not known, not known
> What was coming to be? It was here, in the kitchen, in the passage,
> In the mews in the barn in the byre in the market place
> In our veins our bowels our skulls as well
> As well as in the plottings of potentates
> As well as in the consultations of powers.

Comparison with *The Waste Land* and "The Dry Salvages" shows this chorus as central to the body of Eliot's poetry. Here is "What the Thunder Said": the "Murmur of maternal lamentation," the vision of the dissolution of human order and history, which lead to the Chapel Perilous and the "damp gust/Bringing rain." The opening of "The Dry Salvages" creates much the same feeling of the dissolution of human order and human time. Here the river is a "death-bringer," always involved with man, however remote it may appear. The rhythm, the time kept by the river is equated with the natural flow of man's life from birth to death, as Miss Gardner has said.[4] Miss Gardner has also shown that the movement of the river differs from that of the sea, which is without direction; and this is a crucial distinction in understanding the poem. If man looks beyond the rhythm of his own machines, he can understand the river's movement from source to mouth, which is like the movement from past to future; but when the river, the "brown god," merges with the sea, which contains "Many gods and many voices," man's sense of direction and of time is lost:

> The tolling bell
> Measures time not our time, rung by the unhurried
> Ground swell, a time
> Older than the time of chronometers, older
> Than time counted by anxious worried women
> Lying awake, calculating the future,
> Trying to unweave, unwind, unravel
> And piece together the past and the future. . . .

We watch with wonder the sea and

> Its hints of earlier and other creation:
> The starfish, the hermit crab, the whale's backbone;
> The pools where it offers to our curiosity
> The more delicate algae and the sea anemone.

Here the relation of this *Quartet* to the play becomes clear. The "anxious worried women" are like the Chorus of Women

[4] Helen Gardner, "Four Quartets: A Commentary," in *T. S. Eliot: A Study of His Writings by Several Hands,* ed. B. Rajan (London, Dennis Dobson, 1947), pp. 57-77; see esp. pp. 67-8.

of Canterbury who are attempting to measure events on a human scale, but are dragged, as by the bell tolling with the ground swell, to a bewildering vision of a universe which will not fit into the human order, to a terrifying sense of some relation with the "living things under sea," and finally to a sense of design, not that of past and future, but a design centered upon a timeless moment of illumination, a still point round which the world is ordered: the death of God's martyr, an "instant eternity." The bell of "The Dry Salvages" indicates such a moment, giving significance to a life of which we can otherwise only say, "There is no end, but addition: the trailing/Consequence of further days and hours." The bell, like the death of Becket, is "perpetual angelus," a remembrance of the Incarnation. Through its "symbol perfected in death," the play presents the "end" of man envisaged in "Burnt Norton":

> The inner freedom from the practical desire,
> The release from action and suffering, release from the inner
> And the outer compulsion, yet surrounded
> By a grace of sense, a white light still and moving. . . .

VII

William Carlos Williams: On the Road to Paterson

DURING the years 1946-51 we had the privilege of watching one of the most exhilarating sights in recent literature. A writer over sixty, whose work for nearly forty years had seemed only a series of new starts, burst into a fury of creation that suddenly lifted him to a major place among American writers. This, of course, was not surprising to Dr. Williams: he had always planned to do it as soon as his other essential occupation—his medical practice—would permit. He once explained to a friend, "You see, as a writer I haven't even begun to do anything yet. All I've been able to achieve so far has been survival. . . . I made up my mind that I'd have to live to be very old, like Titian or the Jap whose name I have forgotten, before I should be able to get into that peaceful country where I could sit down to the difficult task of composition." [1] Well, that peaceful country (need we say?) was hard to find. Parents continued to break up his vacation in New England by calling from Denver to ask about a sick child; and in 1950 we still find him interrupting a note with this apology: "23 hours later—15 minutes to myself—one of them used up now: the violence of my life at least serves

[1] *Briarcliff Quarterly*, 3 (1946), 163-4.

to break up some overly devoted moods and give me a fresh start." [2]

Nevertheless, as these remarks indicate, Williams faced the facts of his and our existence with acceptance and toleration—and better still, with amusement and a wry enthusiasm for so live a chaos. He sat down to do what he could, as best he could; and the result, in that short, uneasy wait between wars, was astounding. The year 1950 saw the publication of his collected stories, *Make Light of It*, and his *Collected Later Poems;* the first of these contained twenty-one stories that had not hitherto appeared in any of his books, thirteen of them here printed for the first time; while the second presented a rich and varied collection of about two hundred poems written during the decade of the 1940's. In addition to these we had, at intervals, the four books of his long poem, *Paterson* (1946, 1948, 1949, 1951)—the complete poem, according to Williams' original plan. Also in 1951 came the *Autobiography*, along with a massive reminder of his previous achievement, the *Collected Earlier Poems*, which included his poetry up through 1939. Beyond these demonstrations of power, old and new, we had the play, *A Dream of Love* (1948) and the excellent *Selected Poems* (1949), to say nothing of essays, notes, reviews, and a chapter from the third part of his trilogy of novels.

Through all this apparent welter of production there is an order, a reason, a firm and central purpose to be discerned. An effort to discover this unity might very well begin with the *Selected Poems*, using some of the insights suggested by Randall Jarrell in his witty introduction. For in this volume, certainly, we have a fair sampling of the best among Williams' shorter poems, from his early echoes of Pound, Kreymborg, and Imagism, through the terse lyrics of his middle years, to the more am-

[2] *Modern American Poetry*, ed. B. Rajan (London, Dennis Dobson, 1950), p. 188.

bitious, often sprawling efforts of his later years. The whole volume produces, I think, exactly the effect created by reading the *Collected Later Poems* in the light of Williams' earlier poetry—a sense that, somehow, the poems "lack culmination," as R. P. Blackmur has said.[3] About a quarter of the way through this selection, in the poems from *Spring and All* (1923), we have the sense of a settled achievement, a new form in the short lyric, mastered. The poems that follow do not very often succeed in extending this style: concrete details, presented with spare, terse commentary, in short lines, brief stanzas, clipped, rigorously designed:

> The pure products of America
> go crazy—
> mountain folk from Kentucky
>
> or the ribbed north end of
> Jersey
> with its isolate lakes . . .
>
> No one
> to witness
> and adjust, no one to drive the car.
> (*Spring and All*, poem XVIII)

Here, essentially, is the mode of such later successes as "It Is a Living Coral," "Perpetuum Mobile," or "Burning the Christmas Greens"—and of forty or fifty brief and brilliant pieces in the volume of *Collected Later Poems*.

It is clear, though, that during the 1940's Williams found this style inadequate; he began to reach out for a wider range of reference, a more inclusive and flexible style. "The Clouds" and "The Pink Church" represent violent attempts to break the mould, through abstractions, learned reference, the hieratic

[3] Blackmur, *The Expense of Greatness* (New York, Arrow Editions, 1940), p. 233.

voice; but the seed here dies on what for Williams is barren ground. There is, however, another style in these later poems that, often diffuse, shows a new and fertile direction—a style of easy, rippling, colloquial rumination, very close to prose, but pitched just one tone higher:

> When with my mother I was coming down
> from the country the day of the hurricane,
> trees were across the road and small branches
> kept rattling on the roof of the car
> There was ten feet or more of water
> making the parkways impassible with wind
> bringing more rain in sheets. Brown torrents
> gushed up through new sluices in the
> valley floor . . .
>
> ("The Forgotten City")

That style, we feel, may lead somewhere—but the end is not achieved among these shorter poems; the style of *Spring and All* still dominates.

A review of Williams' earlier volumes of poetry, as they appeared, would, I think, reinforce the impression that this volume of 1923 represents the fulfillment of one cycle in Williams' career. The poems of *Spring and All* come indeed almost with the effect Williams suggests in the spoofing, bombastic prose that introduces them: "Now at last that process of miraculous verisimilitude, that . . . copying which evolution has followed, repeating move for move every move that it made in the past—is approaching the end. Suddenly it is at an end. THE WORLD IS NEW." And the opening poem is, significantly, that old anthology-exhibit, "By the road to the contagious hospital." In many ways this whole volume bears the marks of a new certainty, as compared with the "casual character," the "miscellany" of his five earlier volumes. It was one of these—*Al Que Quiere!* (1917)—that evoked this description of its contents from Wallace Stevens, along with his warning that "to fidget with points of view leads always to new beginnings and incessant new beginnings lead to sterility." [4] But *Spring and All* quiets such misgivings.

The twenty-eight poems of the volume are imbedded in passages of prose criticism that show Williams' theory of poetry—and his view of his own poetry—fully formulated. "I think often of my earlier work and what it has cost me not to have been clear. I acknowledge I have moved chaotically about refusing or rejecting most things." But now, he continues, "I have come to a different condition. I find that the values there discovered can be extended . . . I find that there is work to be done in the creation of new forms, new names for experience and that 'beauty' is related not to 'loveliness' but to a state in which reality plays a part." Reading the original volume, one can feel the honesty and rigor of the critical thinking out of which these poems have grown, while the poems themselves prove the soundness of the theory. Sometimes they seem to sprout directly from the commentary, as with the two poems, "The rose is obsolete" and "The sunlight in a yellow plaque," which are placed in the middle of a discussion—literally in the middle of a sentence—about a picture by Juan Gris. As the prose swirls around these poems we see how both cunningly represent the methods of contemporary painting applied to poetry: "One thing laps over on the other, the cloud laps over on the shutter, the bunch of grapes is part of the handle of the guitar . . . All drawn with admirable simplicity and excellent design—all a unity—" That judgment is true for "The rose is obsolete," but not for the other poem here, which is only a witty exercise, showing the kind of materials that might, theoretically, be set together in this "new form":

[4] See Williams, "Prologue" to *Kora in Hell: Improvisations* (Boston, Four Seas, 1920), pp. 17-18; reprinted in Williams' *Selected Essays* (New York, Random House, 1954).

The sunlight in a
yellow plaque upon the
varnished floor

is full of a song
inflated to
fifty pounds pressure

at the faucet of
June that rings
the triangle of the air

pulling at the
anemonies in
Persephone's cow pasture—

This is the sort of thing that often happens in Williams' poetry—experiments too obviously set to try a theory. But more than half the poems here are certainly successful, though many of them will not appear to full advantage unless the poems are read in their original, numbered sequence. One will note then that the first three poems form a tight triad of spring-songs. First the tenacity of life, human and vegetable, amid the atmosphere of death and disease: the plants are reborn like convalescents emerging from the contagious hospital: both like infants facing the first light:

They enter the new world naked,
cold, uncertain of all
save that they enter. All about them
the cold, familiar wind—

Now the grass, tomorrow
the stiff curl of wildcarrot leaf

One by one objects are defined—
It quickens: clarity, outline of leaf

But now the stark dignity of
entrance—

With Poem II we move indoors to find the potted plant in flower, waiting to be set outdoors. And in III we return to the landscape of Poem I, now completed by the figure of a dominant human creator:

> Down past the brushwood
> bristling by
> the rainsluiced wagonroad
> looms the artist figure of
> the farmer—composing
> —antagonist

Most of the other poems are not by any means so tightly related as the first three; nevertheless, they cling together, through similarity in form, through certain strands of imagery and theme, and through the total pressure of the personality that gives the view,

> in the most practical frame of
> brown celluloid made to
> represent tortoiseshell—
> (Poem X)

One mode, then, has been mastered, but others lie ahead. This, perhaps, is the meaning of the long section at the end of *Spring and All*, where the commentary attempts in many different ways to define the difference between prose and poetry:

prose: statement of facts concerning emotions, intellectual states, data of all sorts—technical expositions, jargon, of all sorts—fictional and other—

poetry: new form dealt with as a reality in itself.

The form of prose is the accuracy of its subject matter—how best to expose the multiform phases of its material

the form of poetry is related to the movements of the imagination revealed in words—or whatever it may be—

the cleavage is complete

In any case, the year 1923 marks such a cleavage in Williams' work, for in this year also appeared his first book of prose-fiction, *The Great American Novel.* From then until 1940, Williams' work in prose almost overwhelmed his output of poetry: three thick novels,[5] a novelette, two volumes of short stories, and his excursion into history, *In the American Grain.*

It is tempting to take the volume of collected stories as an index to Williams' achievement in the realm of prose. But of course it will not work out this way. For the range of the successful stories here is severely limited: the volume, uncannily, produces much the same impression that we had in reading the *Selected Poems.* First, experiments, then mature mastery of a narrow range continued in the best of the later stories. The volume falls into three sections: the stories first collected in *The Knife of the Times* (1932), those that appeared in the larger volume, *Life Along the Passaic River* (1938), and a final section presenting the twenty-one stories not previously collected.[6] The lack of culmination, however, is felt more acutely in this book, for the last section is clearly the least successful of the three. There is no story here that can match the half-dozen perfect stories of *Life Along the Passaic River*, or the best story of the earliest volume, "Old Doc Rivers." The finest stories—and they rank with the best of our time—are all presented in the guise of a doctor's reminiscences, packed with clear and often clinical detail; there is a bareness, a frankness in the language that reveals the narrator's sympathies, starkly, as if by incision: "Jean Beicke," "A Face of Stone," "The Girl with a Pimply Face," "The Use of Force." When all is said, these stories look

[5] A *Voyage to Pagany* (1928), and the first two novels of his trilogy, *White Mule* (1937) and *In the Money* (1940); the third novel of the trilogy, *The Build-Up*, appeared in 1952.

[6] The collection has been republished, with one additional story, under the title *The Farmers' Daughters* (Norfolk, Conn., New Directions, 1961); the long new story, which gives the volume its title, helps to focus the whole volume.

like by-products of the novels, which in turn lack the development that one would expect to see in a major achievement.

More and more, as the books of *Paterson* appeared, all Williams' writings began to look like by-products, preliminary steps, the results of "practicing" (as Wallace Stevens has suggested)[7] for the central work of his career. The title, *Life Along the Passaic River,* is enough to point the way. And now, as one looks back over his shorter poems, anticipations of *Paterson* appear everywhere, even in the early volumes. Thus in *Al Que Quiere!* (1917) we have the long poem, "The Wanderer," containing a section entitled "Paterson—the Strike," from which Williams took four lines almost verbatim to place near the opening of *Paterson II:*

> . . the ugly legs of the young girls,
> pistons too powerful for delicacy! .
> the men's arms, red, used to heat and cold,
> to toss quartered beeves and .

The same poem ends with the speaker's dedication of his talents to "The Passaic, that filthy river":

> Then the river began to enter my heart,
> Eddying back cool and limpid
> Into the crystal beginning of its days.
> But with the rebound it leaped forward:
> Muddy, then black and shrunken . . .

Here, thirty years before, Williams had found his central symbol: the river that courses through and unifies his major poem. In the *Collected Poems* of 1938 we find several excerpts headed "At the Bar: from 'Paterson,'" "Paterson: Episode 17," and so on; most of which later appeared, modified and scattered through the first three books of *Paterson.* And in the *Collected Later Poems* we find the first poem announcing the theme that

[7] See Wallace Stevens' perceptive note, "Rubbings of Reality," in *Briarcliff Quarterly,* 3 (1946), 201-2; included in Stevens' *Opus Posthumous* (New York, Alfred A. Knopf, 1957), pp. 257-9.

rings throughout *Paterson I*: "no ideas but in things"; we find a poem called "Paterson: the Falls," which presents the whole plan of *Paterson* along with numerous phrases echoed in the long poem; and there are other parallels of phrase and theme. It is fair, I think, to see the whole relation of the *Later Poems* to *Paterson* in the light of one significant fact: nine of the poems, here presented independently, appeared in a numbered sequence of *The Broken Span* (1941) under the general title, "For the poem, *Paterson*."

Thus, in his short poems and prose-fiction (and in his plays also, though these are less important) Williams had been discovering his materials, perfecting his technique, waiting for the day when this mastery of prose and poetry could be fused into one major work. But the central principle, the furious heat that makes this fusion ("culmination") possible, cannot be found until we turn to that unique and most significant work of Williams' early career: *In the American Grain* (1925). It is a book that defies classification; but one thing seems certain: these sketches of figures and events in the development of the New World are not to be regarded primarily as "history." Considered historically, the portrait of Columbus may be "true," as the portrait of Aaron Burr is probably "false"; but the work cannot ultimately be judged on such grounds, any more than Shakespeare's *Henry IV* can be so judged. Through the medium of these materials, *In the American Grain* explores the nature of man's fate, presents an attitude toward life, conveys, through historical symbols, the ethical and aesthetic ideals from which Williams' life and work have grown.

The problems are presented in American terms: as problems that confront American writers—and all Americans—in the present. Yet the fundamental problem is universal: how to blend the Old World with the New, how to pass from old ways of thought to new, how to deal with achieved and dying forms amid the active flux of the new and unachieved. *In the Ameri-*

can Grain presents two opposite ways of meeting the problem. One is symbolized in Williams' presentation of the Puritan: the way of those who, being "afraid to touch," set up a "resistance to the wilderness." "Having in themselves nothing of curiosity, no wonder, for the New World—that is nothing official—they knew only to keep their eyes blinded, their tongues in orderly manner between their teeth, their ears stopped by the monotony of their hymns and their flesh covered in straight habits. . . . All that they saw they lived by but denied." [8] Against this creed, with "its rigid clarity," Williams sets another view, represented in a rich array of heroes—men who are aroused by the "wonder" of the new life about them. Columbus, who wrote of his New World as if it were another Eden; De Soto, whose wonder at the new could not be satisfied till he was blended with the mud of the Mississippi's bottom; Raleigh, "seer who failed, planter who never planted," but who knew "shoal water where we smelt so sweet and so strong a smell, as if we had been in the midst of some delicate garden." Or, in a chapter placed between two searing chapters on the Puritans, Champlain: "a man after my own heart," says Williams, "the perfection of what we lack, here," a man whom he describes in words that seem a manifesto of his own ideals: "To me there is a world of pleasure in watching just that Frenchman, just Champlain, like no one else about him, watching, keeping the thing whole within him with almost a woman's tenderness—but such an energy for detail—a love of the exact detail—."

In such heroes we have a sense of wonder quite unlike Cotton Mather's "Wonders of the Invisible World," from which Williams gives us large extracts to set against his accounts of the great explorers. For in Mather's "Wonders" we have a world of perverted detail: observations grotesquely warped to serve a narrow creed: humanity destroyed by false witness. We turn with a shock from these records of the witchcraft trials to the

[8] See the chapter "Père Sebastian Rasles."

chapter headed "Père Sebastian Rasles;" and here, exactly in the middle of the book, its themes and purposes become explicit. Suddenly we are in the Paris of the 'twenties, with Picasso, Braque, and Joyce, with Gertrude, Ezra, and a dozen other expatriates; and Williams is talking at length with Valery Larbaud about the problems facing American writers. Williams is vehement, evangelical: in this ancient scene, where his friends are finding comfort in their exile, Williams (encouraged only by the subtle Frenchman) proclaims a view that looks toward home.

"There is a source *in America* for everything we think or do," he cries. "What has been morally, aesthetically worth while in America has rested upon peculiar and discoverable ground." Then he outlines this "ground" in terms of "two flaming doctrines" that have acted "as contrasting influences in shaping the aesthetic and the moral fiber of the growing race": the Puritan, and its opposite, here represented by Rasles, the French Jesuit who lived among the Indians for thirty-four years, "*touching* them every day." In Rasles, as in his other heroes, Williams finds a spirit "rich, blossoming, generous, able to give and to receive, full of taste, a nose, a tongue, a laugh." This, he declares, is "a moral source not reckoned with, peculiarly sensitive and daring in its close embrace of native things." We can see what it all means, in this Parisian setting: these exiles—are they not the true descendants of the Puritans? "There was no ground to build on, with a ground all blossoming about them—under their noses."

The point is driven home in the next chapter, where, treating "The Discovery of Kentucky," Williams summarizes the issues:

> For the problem of the New World was, as every new comer soon found out, an awkward one, on all sides the same: how to replace from the wild land that which, at home, they had scarcely known the Old World meant to them; through difficulty and even brutal hardship to find a ground to take the place of England. . . .

> Boone's genius was to recognize the difficulty as neither material nor political but one purely moral and aesthetic. Filled with the wild beauty of the New World to overbrimming so long as he had what he desired, to bathe in, to explore always more deeply, to see, to feel, to touch—his instincts were contented.

To be sure, the "orchidean beauty" which Cortez saw in Montezuma's city is gone—destroyed by the attempt to use and dominate, and not simply to feel the new and wonder at its texture. The result, in *Paterson*, is symbolized in the devastated landscape of northern New Jersey, with its "thrashing, breeding, debased city," its incredible mixture of races, its welter of factories mingling with the remnants of aboriginal green: all strewn along the polluted waters of the Passaic. But it is still a new world to be discovered after the manner of Poe, who appears in *In the American Grain* as "a new De Soto," a writer whose greatness lies in the fact that he "faced inland, to originality, with the identical gesture of a Boone."

> He was the first to realize that the hard, sardonic, truculent mass of the New World, hot, angry—was, in fact, not a thing to paint over, to smear, to destroy—for it *would* not be destroyed, it was too powerful,—it smiled! That it is *not* a thing to be slighted by men. Difficult, its very difficulty was their strength. It was in the generous bulk of its animal crudity that their every fineness would be found safely imbedded.

There is the task of *Paterson:* to search out this fineness, this goodness, this "Beautiful Thing," and display it imbedded in all its crudity and truculence.

It was in fact about this time (1925) that plans for *Paterson* began to take shape. Vivienne Koch has found among Williams' manuscripts of this period a significant passage that enables us to see *Paterson* as the product of a plan matured through twenty years of rigorous preparation:

> Note! The conception of a lyric or tragic drama demands lyrics! Studies in language should precede that, the spontaneous . . . as

it is heard. Attempt to feel and then transcribe these lyrical languages in *Paterson*. The drama, the lyric drama (Lope de Vega) should be one expanded metaphor. Poetry demands a different material than prose. It uses another facet of the same fact; . . . Fact, but just before and just after the incident which prose (journalism) would select and by that, miss the significance poetry catches aslant! [9]

"Studies in language . . . as it is heard"—an appropriate description of Williams' stories, and of parts of his novels as well. For many of the stories sound like pages from a writer's (doctor's) journal: conversations, brief anecdotes, whose impact lies in their record of the ring of speech: the Italian, the Negro, the teen-ager, the garage attendant, the steel-worker, the housewife, held tight in the mind, their speech pressing against the language of the doctor-narrator:

I'll see you in a couple of days, I said to them all.

Doctor! the old woman was still after me. You come back. I pay you. But all a time short. Always tomorrow come milk man. Must pay rent, must pay coal. And no got money. Too much work. Too much wash. Too much cook. Nobody help. I don't know what's a matter. This door, doctor, this door. This house make sick. Make sick.

Do the best I can, I said as I was leaving.

("The Girl with a Pimply Face")

It all follows from the glimpse of Williams' methods that we have in a passage of *In the American Grain*, where he quotes a Negro's vivid speech, and comments, "It is water from a spring to talk with him—it is a quality. I wish I might write a book of his improvisations in slang. I wish I might write a play in collaboration with him." And then he adds, "His old man is a different sort: I once made several pages of notes upon his con-

[9] Koch, *William Carlos Williams* (Norfolk, Conn., New Directions, 1950), p. 152.

versation—" (see the chapter, "Advent of the Slaves"). Only one of the short stories is called "Verbal Transcription," but that title, we suspect, would hold for many more.

Remembering the manuscript passage, quoted above, and giving it just a bit more weight than it will bear, may we not say something like this: that in the prose-fiction Williams was "attempting to feel" the speech for *Paterson,* while in the short poems he was practicing how to "transcribe these lyrical languages"? At any rate, *Paterson* consists of intermingled prose and poetry: prose of exactly the two kinds that Williams had trained himself to master. One is the prose of *In the American Grain,* where the flavor of old documents is frequently retained by generous quotation or by subtle imitation: thus the prose of Columbus, of Franklin, of John Paul Jones, of Cotton Mather, all cut their figure in the grain. Just so in *Paterson,* on a local scale, we have quotations from, or subtly archaized imitations of, old records, chiefly newspaper accounts, dealing with events that figure in the grain of northern New Jersey. And along with these, to form a montage of past and present, we have anecdotes and letters representing every level of modern speech, from the almost illiterate ("I know you just about to shot me")—to the intricate letters of the female poet whose appeals to "Dr. P." bulk so large in *Paterson II*. This prose—one "facet of the fact" —is imbedded in and held together by a matrix of poetry that "catches aslant" the significance which "prose (journalism)" misses.

The correlation between prose and poetry is very sharply pointed up in many places. Early in Book I a turgid, archaic piece of prose relates a strange event in 1812, when a minister's wife, viewing the Passaic Falls, somehow plunged to her death in the waters below. Immediately the poetry makes of this a symbol that recurs, a symbol of the death that awaits humanity unless the poet (in us all) can release a redeeming language:

A false language. A true. A false language pouring—a
language (misunderstood) pouring (misinterpreted) without
dignity, without minister, crashing upon a stone ear.

(Book I)

and leaped (or fell) without a
language, tongue-tied
the language worn out

(Book II)

—at the magic sound of the stream
she threw herself upon the bed—
a pitiful gesture! lost among the words:

(Book II)

They plunged, they fell in a swoon .
or by intention, to make an end—

(Book III)

Or the relationship may be one of ironical contrast, as in the central section of Book II, where the poetical sermon of the Evangelist against riches is interlarded with prose-passages telling of Alexander Hamilton's financial schemes for the young republic and of his plans for a "National Manufactory" powered by the Passaic Falls.

The method is made explicit in Book III, where the poet, reading in the city library, finds his symbols growing as he reads:

Old newspaper files,
to find—a child burned in a field,
no language.

And there rises
a counterpart, of reading, slowly, overwhelming
the mind; anchors him in his chair.

Thus in the middle section the central symbol of the book gradually emerges, as the poet reads of a fire that once swept over Paterson, attended by cyclone and flood: these catastrophes become signs of the forces against which man's creative energies fight their stubborn actions, defensive, defeated, or triumphant.

Not all the prose passages are so closely related to the verse as these; yet all serve their function in terms of the big, encompassing symbol of the poem: the roar of the Passaic Falls, representing the reverberations of the daily world (including hints of the past) in the cavernous brain of Paterson, city, man, and poet, as he "lies on his right side, head near the thunder / of the waters filling his dreams!" (Book I)

> Caught (in mind)
> beside the water he looks down, listens!
> But discovers, still, no syllable in the confused
> uproar: missing the sense (though he tries)
> untaught but listening, shakes with the intensity
> of his listening .
>
> (Book II)
>
> Clearly, it is the new, uninterpreted, that
> remoulds the old, pouring down .
>
> (Book II)

It is the roar of life in the mind, "the whole din of fracturing thought," "pouring down"—the last phrase a dozen times repeated and coming to a climax in the lyric that ends Book III:

> The past above, the future below
> and the present pouring down: the roar,
> the roar of the present, a speech—
> is, of necessity, my sole concern .
>
> I must
> find my meaning and lay it, white,
> beside the sliding water: myself—
> comb out the language—or succumb

For there is, as he has suggested at the opening of Book I, a "common language" to be "combed into straight lines/from that rafter of a rock's/lip": a meaning, a poem, "the highest falls," thus presented in a lyric of Book I which implies the whole process of poetic creation:

> Jostled as are the waters approaching
> the brink, his thoughts
> interlace, repel and cut under,
> rise rock-thwarted and turn aside
> but forever strain forward—
>
> they coalesce now
> glass-smooth with their swiftness,
> quiet or seem to quiet as at the close
> they leap to the conclusion and
> fall, fall in air!

So, amid the tales of murdered Indians, feats of diving, witchcraft, a hideous dwarf, industrial power, a dog, a poetess, fire, flood, pearls, and red sandstone—out of it all, yet tight within its texture of reality, flowers the "Beautiful Thing." The meaning of that phrase, the refrain of Book III, can never be abstractly defined: but we grasp its import through concrete scenes ("no ideas but in things"). The old Evangelist of Book II, preaching "in shirtsleeves" to his sparse and listless audience in the park, "calling to the birds and trees," a faded St. Francis. Or, nearby, the man in tweeds, combing the hair of a "new-washed Collie bitch . . . until it lies as he designs, like ripples in white sand giving off its clean-dog odor." In Book III we may find it in the middle of disaster: "Beautiful thing—intertwined with the fire." The Library "aflame"; "An old bottle, mauled by the fire . . . The glass splotched with concentric rainbows";

> the awesome sight of a tin roof (1880)
> entire, half a block long, lifted like a
> skirt, held by the fire—

Or, clearest scene of all, the "Beautiful Thing" that is the woman in the basement (Book III):

> —flat on your back, in a low bed (waiting)
> under the mud plashed windows among the scabrous
> dirt of the holy sheets .
>
> You showed me your legs, scarred (as a child)
> by the whip .

It is, in short, the human spirit, tenacious of its dreams, refusing to submit to squalor or disaster, finding pleasure in the strength of its own perceptions, in its sympathies, its loves, its ability to mold a world in which

> Things, things unmentionable,
> the sink with the waste farina in it and
> lumps of rancid meat, milk-bottle-tops: have
> here a still tranquility and loveliness
> Have here (in his thoughts)
> a complement tranquil and chaste.
>
> (Book I)

Here, then, in this fabric of local associations, is the "reply to Greek and Latin with the bare hands" which Williams promised in the epigraph to *Paterson:* his answer to Pound and Eliot and others who in Williams' view could not see the "ground all blossoming about them," and instead went abroad to seek other modes of redemption. Indeed the wry echo of Eliot's "East Coker" at the very opening of *Paterson*—

> For the beginning is assuredly
> the end—since we know nothing, pure
> and simple, beyond
> our own complexities—

suggests that the four books of *Paterson* may be considered a deliberate counterpart of Eliot's *Quartets:* the eternal Pelagian's answer to the doctrine of original sin. At least, a general comparison with both Pound and Eliot is certainly demanded in these lines toward the end of Book I:

> Moveless
> he envies the men that ran
> and could run off
> toward the peripheries—
> to other centers, direct—
> for clarity (if
> they found it)
>   loveliness and
> authority in the world—
>
> a sort of springtime
> toward which their minds aspired
> but which he saw,
> within himself—ice bound

Williams knew very well what Eliot had been doing; he (quite grudgingly) respected Eliot as poet and sized him up carefully, as one estimates a strong opponent in the ring. That early tirade in *Improvisations* (1920) was, as Miss Koch has pointed out,[10] an attack not so much on Eliot as on the British critic who had held up Prufrock as a "New World type," and had called "La Figlia" the "very fine flower of the finest spirit of the United States." Williams read these poems with great insight: "Prufrock, the nibbler at sophistication, endemic in every capital . . . I cannot question Eliot's observation. Prufrock is a masterly portrait . . . but the type is universal." As for the New World, Williams added, it is "Montezuma or since he was stoned to death in a parley, Guatemozin who had the city of Mexico levelled over him before he was taken." The point is that, for Williams, this was not American poetry—it did not present a way that American writers should follow. A page or so later he says pretty much the same thing about his friend Ezra Pound: "E. P. is the best enemy United States verse has. . . . He does

[10] Koch, pp. 30-31; see "Prologue" to *Kora in Hell*, pp. 25-8.

not, however, know everything, not by more than half. The accordances of which Americans have the parts and the colors but not the completions before them pass beyond the attempts of his thought." We can understand, then, the tartness of the tone with which in 1950 he answered a British questionnaire about American poetry: "Eliot's work stopped the development of American poetry for over twenty years by the tremendous popular success of its mannerisms. His influence here today is paltry though there is no one in America who does not acknowledge his skill or in fact who does not take pleasure in his successes. We have learned, however, not to be thrown off our gait by him." [11]

Williams fairly analysed this whole issue in his "Letter to an Australian Editor," [12] one of his best critical pieces, perceptive, tentative, ramifying, in the way of Eliot's better essays. It is mainly an attempt to explain, Williams says, "how diametrically I am opposed (in my work) to such a writer as Ezra Pound—whom I love and deeply admire." Williams here sets up two kinds of poets. The first consists of those who "think in terms of the direct descent of great minds," who feel a "mind to mind fertilization" arising from their massive reading in past writers; these men tend to compose "in the forms of the past and even when they deviate from the fixed classic forms it is nevertheless precisely the established and accepted work of the masters from which they consciously deviate, by which they are asserting their greatest originality." (Note the parallel with Eliot's "Tradition and the Individual Talent.") But there is also another kind of poet, "another literary source continuing the greatness of the past which does not develop androgynetically from the past itself mind to mind but from the present," a poet for whom both the fertility and the forms of his art "arise from the society about him of which he is (if he is to be fed) a part—the fecundating

[11] *Modern American Poetry*, ed. Rajan, p. 189.
[12] *Briarcliff Quarterly*, 3 (1946), 205-8.

men and women about him who have given him birth."

It is a helpful distinction to recall as we read and re-read the *Quartets*, the *Cantos*, and *Paterson*. For Williams' achievement, in its own way, deserves the tribute of this company.

VIII

William Carlos Williams: Inventions for the Loom

> and as for the solidity of the white oxen in all this
> perhaps only Dr Williams (Bill Carlos)
> will understand its importance,
> its benediction. He wd/have put in the cart.
>
> Pound, Canto 78

THROUGHOUT the books of *Paterson* the presence of Ezra Pound has become more and more significant, more and more explicit. After the hints of a difference in aim in Book I, we find that difference subtly suggested in a passage of Book II, where Williams seems to echo wryly one of the most famous passages of Pound, Canto 45, on usury, where Pound adopts the manner of a medieval or a renaissance preacher:

> With usura hath no man a house of good stone
> each block cut smooth and well fitting
> that design might cover their face,
> with usura
> hath no man a painted paradise on his church wall
> *harpes et luthes* . . .
>
> with usura the line grows thick
> with usura is no clear demarcation
> and no man can find site for his dwelling.
> Stone cutter is kept from his stone
> weaver is kept from his loom . . .

> Came not by usura Angelico; came not Ambrogio Praedis,
> Came no church of cut stone signed: *Adamo me fecit* . . .
>
> Usura rusteth the chisel
> It rusteth the craft and the craftsman
> It gnaweth the thread in the loom
> None learneth to weave gold in her pattern . . .

And now this from *Paterson:*

> Without invention nothing is well spaced,
> unless the mind change, unless
> the stars are new measured, according
> to their relative positions, the
> line will not change . . .
>
> without invention
> nothing lies under the witch-hazel
> bush, the alder does not grow from among
> the hummocks margining the all
> but spent channel of the old swale,
> the small foot-prints
> of the mice under the overhanging
> tufts of the bunch-grass will not
> appear: without invention the line
> will never again take on its ancient
> divisions when the word, a supple word,
> lived in it, crumbled now to chalk.

What does this contrast say of these two poets at their best? Williams' own critical acuteness gives us the answer in one of his letters of 1932:

> So far I believe that Pound's line in his *Cantos*—there is something *like* what we shall achieve. Pound in his mould, a medieval inspiration, patterned on a substitution of medieval simulacra for a possible, not yet extant modern and living material, has made a pre-composition for us. Something which when later (perhaps) packed and realized in living, breathing stuff will (in its changed form) be the thing.[1]

[1] *The Selected Letters of William Carlos Williams,* ed. John C. Thirlwall (New York, McDowell, Obolensky, 1957), p. 135.

It is a summary of Williams' achievement in *Paterson:* the mold is Pound's, combining verse and prose; the line is Pound's, with its flexible cadences, breaking the pentameter; but everything is altered through Williams' invention, his conviction that bold exploration of the local will result in the discovery of a new world blossoming all about him. Pound's mind lives at its best among the splendors of ancient human artifacts, and when these splendors seem threatened, Pound seeks a social answer. He seeks to make art possible by reforming the economic basis of society. It is a difference between the two friends that Pound has acutely described in his essay on Williams (1928), as he contrasts their two temperaments: "If he wants to 'do' anything about what he sees, this desire for action does not rise until he has meditated in full and at leisure. Where I see scoundrels and vandals, he sees a spectacle or an ineluctable process of nature. Where I want to kill at once, he ruminates." [2]

At the same time, in his ruminative way, Williams gradually implies some degree of sympathy with Pound's economic views. Among the prose passages of the second book of *Paterson,* we find attacks on the Federal Reserve System; we find, too, implied attacks on Alexander Hamilton's plans for federal financing and for creating a great "National Manufactory." These prose excerpts on financial matters are interwoven with the poetical sermon of the evangelist who, in the second book of *Paterson,* delivers his sermon against money to the birds and trees of the park. But this financial theme, thus introduced, is tightly contained within this section: it lies there dormant, recessive, exerting a tacit pressure on the landscape, until, in the center of Book IV, it bursts out again in a highly Poundian diatribe beginning "Money: Joke." Here is a section composed in something like Pound's broken multi-cultural style, with expressions in Hebrew, Spanish, and German, along with very crude American

[2] *Literary Essays of Ezra Pound,* ed. T. S. Eliot (London, Faber & Faber, 1954), p. 392.

slang; and including too some allusions to the Parthenon, Phidias, and Pallas Athene—all this ending with an overt echo of Pound's unmistakable epistolary style:

IN
venshun.
O.KAY
In venshun

(It sounds like Pound nodding his head to the passage on invention that I have just quoted.)

and seeinz az how yu hv/started. Will you consider
a remedy of a lot:
I.E. LOCAL control of local purchasing
power .
? ?
Difference between squalor of spreading slums
and splendor of renaissance cities.

It is a tribute to Pound, yes; but it is not for Williams to conclude his own poem in this foreign vein, it is not for Williams to excoriate the present and celebrate the "splendor of renaissance cities." This is the kind of invitation that Williams has already refused to accept in the third book of *Paterson*, entitled "The Library," where we find the poet attempting to discover a "sanctuary to our fears" amid the "cool of books":

A cool of books
will sometimes lead the mind to libraries
of a hot afternoon, if books can be found
cool to the sense to lead the mind away.

He is attempting to escape from the roar of the Falls, for that roar in his mind, "pouring down," has left him exhausted.

. . . a falls unseen
tumbles and rights itself
and refalls—and does not cease, falling
and refalling with a roar, a reverberation
not of the falls but of its rumor
unabated

Here, the mysterious evocative symbol of the great Falls of the Passaic comes as close to clarity as we shall ever find it. It seems to represent the roar of language coming down from the past, mingling with the present, and now bursting downward over the brain of "Paterson," who seeks to find somehow, in that fall of speech, the beautiful thing that is the ground of his desire. "What do I do? I listen, to the water falling. . . . This is my entire occupation." But now he is

> Spent from wandering the useless
> streets these months, faces folded against
> him like clover at nightfall,

and he feels that somehow

> Books will give rest sometimes against
> the uproar of water falling
> and righting itself to refall filling
> the mind with its reverberation.

But it is not so. As he sits there reading old annals of Paterson, he finds the roar there, too: stories of fire, cyclone, and flood that now beset the poet until his mind "reels, starts back amazed from the reading," until the very poem threatens to break apart upon the page.[3] Where to turn? What to do? In ironical answer, Williams brings in certain excerpts from a letter headed "S. Liz," that is, from St. Elizabeth's Hospital:

> re read *all* the Gk tragedies in
> Loeb.—plus Frobenius, plus Gesell.
> plus Brooks Adams
> ef you ain't read him all.—
> Then Golding's Ovid is in
> Everyman's lib.
>
> & nif you want a readin
> list ask papa—but don't
> go rushin to *read* a book

[3] See *Paterson* (New York, New Directions, 1963), p. 164.

just cause it is mentioned
eng passang—is fraugs.

"That's French." Williams' answer to Pound's ribbing is sly. On the next page, he prints an excerpt from some record evidently found in the Paterson Library concerning the drillings taken at the artesian well of the Passaic Rolling Mill, Paterson. As the results of this local rock-drill run down the page, the excerpt concludes with this significant suggestion: "The fact that the rock salt of England, and of some of the other salt mines of Europe, is found in rocks of the same age as this, raises the question whether it may not also be found here."

"Whether it may not also be found here." For Williams, it may and it will be found here, as he proves by giving in the final section of Book IV a recovery of the source: the pastoral Paterson of early days at peace with the Falls.

In a deep-set valley between hills, almost hid
by dense foliage lay the little village.
Dominated by the Falls the surrounding country
was a beautiful wilderness where mountain pink
and wood violet throve: a place inhabited only
by straggling trappers and wandering Indians.

* * * * *

Just off Gun Mill yard, on the gully
was a long rustic winding stairs leading
to a cliff on the opposite side of the river.
At the top was Fyfield's tavern—watching
the birds flutter and bathe in the little
pools in the rocks formed by the falling
mist—of the Falls . . .

Here is our home, says the poet, inland by the Falls and not in the outgoing sea, as Williams concludes in the rousing finale of Book IV:

I warn you, the sea is *not* our home.
the sea is not our home

Here the sea appears to symbolize something more than simple death, national or personal annihilation. For this is also a sea where "float words, snaring the seeds":

> the nostalgic sea
> sopped with our cries
> Thalassa! Thalassa!
> calling us home .
> I say to you, Put wax rather in your
> ears against the hungry sea
> it is not our home!
> . draws us in to drown, of losses
> and regrets .

The sea appears to represent the pull of longing toward a lost culture, a pull outward from the source, as he goes on to indicate by an overwrought cry that seems to parody the longing of a Pound or an Eliot:

> Oh that the rocks of the Areopagus had
> kept their sounds, the voices of the law!
> Or that the great theatre of Dionysius
> could be aroused by some modern magic
>
> * * * * *
>
> Thalassa! Thalassa!
> Drink of it, be drunk!
> Thalassa
> immaculata: our home, our nostalgic
> mother in whom the dead, enwombed again
> cry out to us to return .

". . . not our home!" cries the poet again in violent protest, "It is NOT our home." And suddenly at the very close of this fourth book, the scene shifts, the tone shifts, to a common seashore with a man bathing in the sea, and his dog waiting for him on the beach.

> When he came out, lifting his knees
> through the waves she went to him frisking
> her rump awkwardly .

Wiping his face with his hand he turned
to look back to the waves, then
knocking at his ears, walked up
to stretch out flat on his back in
the hot sand .

And finally after a brief nap and a quick dressing, the man

turned again
to the water's steady roar, as of a distant
waterfall . Climbing the
bank, after a few tries, he picked
some beach plums from a low bush and
sampled one of them, spitting the seed out,
then headed inland, followed by the dog

"Headed inland"—here at the very close, Williams echoes his prose preparation for this poem, *In the American Grain,* for in the closing pages of that earlier book, he had used similar phrasing to describe the achievement of Edgar Allan Poe. "His greatness," Williams there declared, "is in that he turned his back" upon everything represented by a Longfellow and "faced inland, to originality." And indeed Williams' account here of Poe's method in his tales is perhaps the best account of *Paterson* that we have yet received:

the significance and the secret is: authentic particles, a thousand of which spring to the mind for quotation, taken apart and reknit with a view to emphasize, enforce and make evident, the *method.* Their quality of skill in observation, their heat, local verity, being *overshadowed* only by the detached, the abstract, the cold philosophy of their joining together; a method springing so freshly from the local conditions which determine it, by their emphasis of firm crudity and lack of coordinated structure, as to be worthy of most painstaking study.

II

Steadily, tenaciously, amid the demands of a medical career, the books of *Paterson* appeared, and in 1951 the promised four books thus stood complete, fulfilling the early dedication of "The Wanderer," and carrying out exactly the four-part invention announced in the first edition of Book I:

This is the first part of a long poem in four parts—that a man in himself is a city beginning, seeking, achieving and concluding his life in ways which the various aspects of a city may embody—if imaginatively conceived—any city, all the details of which may be made to voice his most intimate convictions. Part One introduces the elemental character of the place. The Second Part will comprise the modern replicas. Three will seek a language to make them vocal, and Four, the river below the falls, will be reminiscent of episodes—all that any one man may achieve in a lifetime.

No wonder, then, that some admirers of *Paterson* were struck with consternation and dismay, a few years later, at the news that a *fifth* book of *Paterson* was in progress! That four-part design, so carefully announced and explained on several occasions—was it to be discarded now? To say the least, the whole procedure showed little consideration for those critics who had published explanations of the poem's symmetry, and indeed gave encouragement to those who had felt that Book IV did not fulfill the poem's brilliant beginning. But when, in 1958, the threatened Book V at last appeared, it seemed rather like an epilogue or coda, for it was much shorter than the other books, and it was written in a highly reminiscent mode that served to recapitulate and bind together all the foregoing poem. As Williams says in a letter cited on the dust jacket of Book V: "I have come to understand not only that many changes have occurred in me and the world, but I have been forced to recognize that there can be no end to such a story I have envisioned with the terms which I had laid down for myself. I had to take the world of Paterson into a new dimension if I wanted to give it imaginative validity. Yet I wanted to keep it whole, as it is to me." The wholeness of which he speaks is highly personal, in the manner of *Leaves of Grass, Don Juan,* or *The Prelude:* the "epic" of the Romantic self that knows no formal ending, no classical symmetry. At his death, in 1963, Williams was at work on a sixth book of *Paterson*.

Yet as it stands now the poem has a wholeness of the kind that Williams implies and illustrates in Book V. The chief symbol of that wholeness is one that may at first seem incongruous with Williams' lifetime dedication to the local, his persistent refusal to adopt or approve the learned, foreign allusions of Ezra Pound or T. S. Eliot: in Book V the organizing symbol is the series of matchless tapestries in The Cloisters representing "The Hunt of the Unicorn." True, Williams had dealt briefly with these tapestries in the third book of *Paterson:*

> A tapestry hound
> with his thread teeth drawing crimson from
> the throat of the unicorn

But there the allusion to the world of traditional art seemed ironically overwhelmed by the surrounding scenes of basement ugliness and the fighting between "the guys from Paterson" and "the guys from Newark." Literally, it is only a short drive from Paterson to The Cloisters—yet the gap of nearly five hundred years, the distance from France to the Passaic—these are dimensions strange to Williams, however familiar they may be to Pound or Eliot. But an afternoon spent with the great tapestries will show once more the canniness and subtlety of Williams' poetical strategies in *Paterson*.

Williams is defending and explaining his own technique by suggesting an analogy with the mode of the tapestries; and however unlikely any similarity may at first appear, the essential kinship is truly there. For these tapestries, like *Paterson,* achieve their success through a peculiar combination of the local and the mythical. We have the one hundred and one trees, shrubs, herbs, and flowers so realistically woven that eighty-five of them have been identified by botanists and praised for the exactitude of their reproduction; the "millefleurs background" is not composed of merely symbolical designs, but the colors burst forth from the actual, recognizable violet, cornflower, daisy, calendula, or dandelion. Yet all this actuality serves to border and center the mythical beast of oriental legend, serves to enfold and surround the human figures, the dogs, birds, and wild beasts, the castles and streams, the spears and hunting horns that crowd the scenes with a happy disregard of perspective—even to the point where the sixth tapestry superimposes the wounding of the unicorn upon an upper corner of the larger scene where the mythical beast is presented dead before the King and Queen. Meanwhile, amid the brilliant distortions of art and the splendor of color in flowers and costume, we find the brutal faces of certain varlets, the dog gutted by the unicorn's horn, the dog biting the unicorn's back, the vicious spears stabbing the "milk-white beast," the slanting, provocative, betraying eyes of the female attendant upon the virgin.

. cyclamen, columbine, if the art
with which these flowers have been
put down is to be trusted—and
again oak leaves and twigs
that brush the deer's antlers . .
the brutish eyes of the deer
not to be confused
with the eyes of the Queen
are glazed with death .

* * * * *

a tapestry
silk and wool shot with silver threads
a milk white one horned beast
I, Paterson, the King-self
saw the lady
through the rough woods
outside the palace walls

among the stench of sweating horses
and gored hounds
yelping with pain
the heavy breathing pack
to see the dead beast
brought in at last
across the saddle bow
among the oak trees.

The placing of that line, "I, Paterson, the King-self," implies a parallel between "Paterson," the poet, man, self, and city of the poem, and the Unicorn. The mythical beast is the spirit of the imagination, the immortal presence of art:

The Unicorn
has no match
or mate . the artist
has no peer .

So through art alone, male and female, a field of
flowers, a tapestry, spring flowers unequaled
in loveliness.
through this hole
at the bottom of the cavern
of death, the imagination
escapes intact
he bears a collar round his neck
hid in the bristling hair.

Thus in the last of the series, the most famous of the tapestries, the Unicorn appears in peaceful resurrection. So "Paterson" now writes "In old age"—the opening line of Book V—and knows the threat of mortality as well as the reassurance promised by everything that the Unicorn represents—as we learn from the long closing passage dominated by the tapestries:

—the aging body
with the deformed great-toe nail

makes itself known
coming
to search me out—with a
rare smile
among the thronging flowers of that field
where the Unicorn
is penned by a low
wooden fence
in April!

* * * * *

the cranky violet
like a knight in chess,
the cinque-foil,
yellow faced—
this is a French
or Flemish tapestry—
the sweetsmelling primrose
growing close to the ground, that poets
have made famous in England,
I cannot tell it all:

* * * * *

Yellow centers, crimson petals
and the reverse,
dandelion, love-in-a-mist,
corn flowers,
thistle and others
the names and perfumes I do not know.
The woods are filled with holly
(I have told you, this
is a fiction, pay attention),
the yellow flag of the French fields is here
and a congeries of other flowers
as well: daffodils
and gentian, the daisy, columbine
petals
myrtle, dark and light
and calendulas .

Anyone who reads the excellent pamphlet on the flora of the tapestries provided by the museum[4] will see at once that most of the flowers here included by Williams are clearly recognizable and listed under these names; but the poet is recreating the act of personal, immediate, imaginative apprehension. Thus at times the poet gives his own familiar names, draws his own conclusions, imagines likenesses. The "myrtle, dark and light," for instance, must be the "periwinkle (*Vinca*)" which "appears only in the two normal colors of white and blue." And the "cinque-foil,/yellow faced" is not mentioned in the museum's account, but it is not hard to find it suggested by certain flowers. Most important, the familiar, intimate quality of the poet's account reminds us that many of these flowers have appeared in the dozens of flower-poems and the hundreds of flower-images scattered throughout the poetry of William Carlos Williams, from his early tributes to the daisy, the primrose, and the "yellow cinquefoil," down through the great tribute to Demuth, "The Crimson Cyclamen," and on into the long flower-tribute to his wife, "Asphodel, That Greeny Flower," where the poet recalls his boyhood collection of "pressed flowers." Williams is one of the great poets of flowers and foliage, which he observes and represents with a loving and a scientific accuracy akin to that of the Unicorn tapestries. In a passage typical of *Paterson's* mode of organization, this fifth book itself reminds us from the outset of the poet's love of flowers by including on its fourth page a personal letter to "Dear Bill":

> I wish you and F. could have come. It was a grand day and we missed you two, one and all missed you. Forgetmenot, wild columbine, white and purple violets, white narcissus, wild anemonies and yards and yards of delicate wild windflowers along the brook showed up at their best. . . .

[4] E. J. Alexander and Carol H. Woodward, *The Flora of the Unicorn Tapestries*, 2nd edn. (The New York Botanical Garden, 1947).

How lovely to read your memories of the place; a place is made of them as well as the world around it. Most of the flowers were put in many years ago and thrive each spring, the wild ones in some new spot that is exciting to see. Hepaticas and bloodroot are now all over the place, and the trees that were infants are now tall creatures filled this season with orioles, some rare warbler like the Myrtle and magnolia warblers and a wren has the best nest in the garage. . . .

So Book V suggests that we might regard *Paterson* as a kind of tapestry, woven out of memories and observations, composed by one man's imagination, but written in part by his friends, whose letters are scattered throughout, by his patients, whose words are remembered throughout, and by all the milling populace of Paterson, past and present, including that unicorn in the center of the field: the King-self, within whose mind these thoughts assemble like

> A flight of birds, all together,
> seeking their nests in the season . . .
>
> The
> colors of their plumage are undecipherable
> in the sun's glare against the sky
> but the old man's mind is stirred
> by the white, the yellow, the black
> as if he could see them there.
>
> Their presence in the air again
> calms him. Though he is approaching
> death he is possessed by many poems.

IX

Theodore Roethke:
A Greenhouse Eden

All appeared New, and Strange at the first, inexpressibly rare, and Delightfull, and Beautifull. . . .

Boys and Girles Tumbling in the Street, and Playing, were moving Jewels. I knew not that they were Born or should Die. . . . Eternity was Manifest in the Light of the Day, and som thing infinit Behind evry thing appeared: which talked with my Expectation and moved my Desire.

The first Light which shined in my Infancy in its Primitiv and Innocent Clarity was totally ecclypsed: insomuch that I was fain to learn all again.

Thomas Traherne, *Centuries*

I HAD been reading Traherne in the daytime, for another purpose, and reading Roethke at night, thinking of this essay. Gradually, almost imperceptibly, the two writers seemed to be flowing together, especially in the sequence of meditative poems, growing out of Eliot's *Quartets,* that open Roethke's posthumous volume, *The Far Field.* This "North American Sequence" begins, as Traherne's meditations begin, with "The Longing" for a lost happiness:

> How comprehensive that felicity! . . .
> A body with the motion of a soul.

* * * * *

The light cries out, and I am there to hear—
I'd be beyond; I'd be beyond the moon,
Bare as a bud, and naked as a worm.

* * * * *

I would with the fish, the blackening salmon, and the mad
lemmings,
The children dancing, the flowers widening.

There are of course the important differences: Traherne's images of light, childhood, and nature, his explorations of the memory, are based upon a firmly argued structure of Augustinian and Platonic thought; while Roethke's use of these images derives from the discoveries of modern psychology, and his method of exploration is based upon the cultivation of the irrational nuance, the fleeting association. Traherne's writings are rational, didactic, doctrinal, and indeed his poetry often suffers badly from an excess of abstraction; whereas Roethke's poetry evades the rational and tends to strip away abstractions. Yet a common origin of strength is there: the belief that in the depths of the self lies a core of power, a source of light, a redemptive memory—although, as Roethke says, in his poetry "The redeemer comes a dark way."

Thus, in the second poem of this new sequence, "Meditation at Oyster River," the mind moves backward from the present scene, as the speaker watches "the first tide-ripples, moving, almost without sound, toward me." In this quiet, even the gulls make no sound,

Their cat-mewing over,
Their child-whimpering.

At last one long undulant ripple,
Blue-black from where I am sitting,
Makes almost a wave over a barrier of small stones,
Slapping lightly against a sunken log.
I dabble my toes in the brackish foam sliding forward,

> Then retire to a rock higher up on the cliff-side.
> The wind slackens, light as a moth fanning a stone:
> A twilight wind, light as a child's breath
> Turning not a leaf, not a ripple.

The imagery of childhood prepares the way for the rippling flood of memory, "The tongues of water, creeping in, quietly."

> I shift on my rock, and I think:
> Of the first trembling of a Michigan brook in April,
> Over a lip of stone, the tiny rivulet;
> And that wrist-thick cascade tumbling from a cleft rock,
> Its spray holding a double rain-bow in early morning,
> Small enough to be taken in, embraced, by two arms,—

and of the frozen river, its ice piled against a bridge, until a blast breaks the jam "And the whole river begins to move forward, its bridges shaking." So the poem ends, with morning recovered at evening, and the spirit freed for its inward explorations:

> Now, in this waning of light,
> I rock with the motion of morning . . .
> Water's my will, and my way,
> And the spirit runs, intermittently,
> In and out of the small waves,
> Runs with the intrepid shorebirds—
> How graceful the small before danger!

The third poem, "Journey to the Interior," moves through arid memories of the deserts and prairies of the American West and Midwest toward the rich recovery of the fourth poem, "The Long Waters," where the speaker returns to the seaside imagery of "Oyster River" and sees

> in the advancing and retreating waters
> The shape that came from my sleep, weeping:
> The eternal one, the child, the swaying vine branch,
> The numinous ring around the opening flower . . .

The mind is on the verge of its deepest discovery, which now is accomplished in the long, intimate memories of childhood that cover more than forty lines of the title poem, "The Far Field," where the mind recovers completely its early sense of unity with natural things:

I suffered for birds, for young rabbits caught in the mower,
My grief was not excessive.
For to come upon warblers in early May
Was to forget time and death:
How they filled the oriole's elm, a twittering restless cloud, all one
morning,
And I watched and watched till my eyes blurred from the bird
shapes,—
Cape May, Blackburnian, Cerulean,—
Moving, elusive as fish, fearless,
Hanging, bunched like young fruit, bending the end branches. . . .

Such images, mingling child, bird, fish, and fruit, represent, as the speaker says at the close of this poem:

The pure serene of memory in one man,—
A ripple widening from a single stone. . . .

The final poem, "The Rose," is perhaps related to Eliot's various rose images; indeed the connotations seem inevitable in view of the many, apparently deliberate, echoes of the *Quartets* that run throughout this sequence, beginning with the question at the end of "The Longing," "Old men should be explorers?" In many ways the whole of "North American Sequence" might be said to represent a sustained tribute to Eliot's example; the sequence has, at any rate, absorbed the method of the *Quartets* and, working within its own free texture of associations, moves toward a moment of the rose where the present flower in its setting of "wind-warped madronas" may evoke the roses in the childhood Eden:

And I think of roses, roses,
White and red, in the wide six-hundred-foot greenhouses,
And my father standing astride the cement benches,

Lifting me high over the four-foot stems, the Mrs. Russells, and
his own elaborate hybrids,
And how those flowerheads seemed to flow toward me, to beckon
me, only a child, out of myself.

One would hardly have expected this conclusion, knowing the Roethke of the early 1930's, with his efforts in the current "metaphysical" mode, his admiration for Donne and Marvell, for conceits such as this, from Marvell's "The Unfortunate Lover":

Till at the last the master-Wave
Upon the Rock his Mother drave;
And there she split against the Stone,
In a *Cesarian Section.*

—a passage that he read gleefully to his classes in 1932. Along with these enthusiasms went, of course, an admiration for Tate and Ransom, for the Elinor Wylie of *Angels and Earthly Creatures*, for the taut lyrics of Louise Bogan's *Body of this Death*; for the young Kunitz of *Intellectual Things*; for authors in the metaphysical mode now almost forgotten, such as Alan Porter in *The Signature of Pain*; and indeed for all the sort of poetry represented in Genevieve Taggard's superb anthology of metaphysical verse, *Circumference*, which he greatly admired. The world of metaphor that Roethke then frequented may be illustrated by a query he used to quote from Louise Bogan: "I wonder," she asked, according to Roethke, "I wonder whether time moves from right to left, or from left to right?"

The early harvest of these admirations is found in his first volume, *Open House* (1941), where the dominant mode is the tersely phrased, strictly metered lyric in quatrains or couplets, often reminiscent of Emily Dickinson; and the chief aim is summed up in the words the publisher used in 1930 to describe the poems in Kunitz's *Intellectual Things*: "these poems express ideas as hard and glittering as quartz." Such is the mode of Roethke's poem "The Adamant":

Thought does not crush to stone.
The great sledge drops in vain.
Truth never is undone;
Its shafts remain.

The teeth of knitted gears
Turn slowly through the night,
But the true substance bears
The hammer's weight.

Compression cannot break
A center so congealed:
The tool can chip no flake;
The core lies sealed.

This is precisely the kind of poem that Miss Taggard was describing in 1929, in her lively preface to *Circumference:* "Ideas being for this temperament as real as grass blades or locomotives, the poet's imagination is always riding the two horses in the circus, Idea and Fact; they gallop neck and neck in his work, he has a genius for both the concrete word and the dazzling concept." "To give an idea no form but itself, to show it as organic by an inner music, as if the bones of a skeleton were singing in their own rhythm—that is the technical obsession of the metaphysical poet." Something of this sort is found in the promise of the title poem in *Open House:*

I'm naked to the bone,
With nakedness my shield.
Myself is what I wear:
I keep the spirit spare.

Yet along with these attractive poems in the current mode one finds the presence of another way in the nature-poems that make up a third of this volume. These too are somewhat metaphysical, in Miss Taggard's terms, echoing Emily Dickinson, Léonie Adams, and the early Frost; but they have nevertheless a quality that we can now see reaching toward another dimension. The celebration of the naked bone, the spare spirit, and the sealed core is not the central mode of Roethke; it is indeed the very opposite of his true motion, which is to unseal, to let flow forth, to nourish into growth, after the manner prefigured in his early poem "The Light Comes Brighter":

> And soon a branch, part of a hidden scene,
> The leafy mind, that long was tightly furled,
> Will turn its private substance into green,
> And young shoots spread upon our inner world.

One poem, above all, in *Open House* suggests a way out of this metaphysical sealing: it is the poem aptly entitled "The Premonition," which Roethke did not choose to include in his volumes of collected, or selected, verse of 1953 and 1958:

> Walking this field I remember
> Days of another summer.
> Oh that was long ago! I kept
> Close to the heels of my father,
> Matching his stride with half-steps
> Until we came to a river.
> He dipped his hand in the shallow:
> Water ran over and under
> Hair on a narrow wrist bone;
> His image kept following after,—
> Flashed with the sun in the ripple.
> But when he stood up, that face
> Was lost in a maze of water.

One can guess why Roethke did not include the poem, for it is quite unlike anything else in this early volume: the frank reminiscence, the utter naturalness and simplicity of the language, the subtle use of terminal assonance (especially of the "er" sound) in place of formal rhyme; the shimmer of implication in place of the hard conceit; the evocation of a mystery instead of the sharp precision of idea. Roethke was in fact embarrassed by the open display of feeling here; ten or fifteen years ago, in discussing this poem, he said that he winced in reading that cry,

"Oh that was long ago!" The exact word he used, I think, was "corny." But now this seems the one poem of *Open House* that clearly points the way home, to Roethke's truest manner, the cultivation of the inner force of memory. It points to the greenhouse memories that form the still point of his deepest imaginative existence, and it finds its fulfillment in Roethke's posthumous volume, in the poem entitled simply "Otto"—his father's name, the name of the greenhouse owner, protector and procreator of greenness:

> He was the youngest son of a strange brood,
> A Prussian who learned early to be rude
> To fools and frauds: He does not put on airs
> Who lived above a potting shed for years.
> I think of him, and I think of his men,
> As close to him as any kith or kin.
> Max Laurisch had the greenest thumb of all.
>
> * * * * *
>
> A house for flowers! House upon house they built,
> Whether for love or out of obscure guilt
> For ancestors who loved a warlike show,
> Or Frenchmen killed a hundred years ago,
> And yet still violent men, whose stacked-up guns
> Killed every cat that neared their pheasant runs;
>
> * * * * *
>
> In my mind's eye I see those fields of glass,
> As I looked out at them from the high house,
> Riding beneath the moon, hid from the moon,
> Then slowly breaking whiter in the dawn;
> When George the watchman's lantern dropped from sight
> The long pipes knocked: it was the end of night.
> I'd stand upon my bed, a sleepless child
> Watching the waking of my father's world.—
> O world so far away! O my lost world!

In this final stanza, with its appropriate echo of Thomas's "Fern Hill" (Roethke's echoes of contemporary poets are, I think, nearly always deliberate and functional), Roethke overcomes his embarrassment at open exclamation: the cry is the full recognition of his true center, bursting out of this poem's Yeatsian mode, as earlier the cry of "The Premonition" had burst out of the metaphysical.

Roethke's development shows that there is no necessary relation between the metaphysical style and the genre of meditative poetry. The two modes co-existed, happily, in the early part of the seventeenth century, but in Vaughan and Traherne we can see that co-existence fading: as with Roethke, the metaphysical style in these two writers is overlaid upon a hidden center. The metaphysical mode of "wit," the "strong lines," the firm intellectual control, which Yeats re-created in his later poetry and which Roethke imitated successfully in his Yeatsian period of the 1950's—this mode of writing is not essential to meditative poetry, though it may help to cultivate that kind of poetry in some eras and in some poets. But there are other ways, and for Roethke the best way was found in the poems of *The Lost Son* (1948)—a volume of great beauty, in its individual poems, in its ordering, in its development, even in the fine pastel-drawing by Charles Seide that graces the jacket: a green stem or twig or shoot, faintly suggesting a rivulet, emerges out of dark patches into a green light, all symbolizing the implications of the volume, as suggested by the second poem, "Cuttings":

> I can hear, underground, that sucking and sobbing,
> In my veins, in my bones I feel it,—
> The small waters seeping upward,
> The tight grains parting at last.
> When sprouts break out,
> Slippery as fish,
> I quail, lean to beginnings, sheath-wet.

The poems of the greenhouse sequence (part I of the volume) move from the darkness of underground, as in "Root Cellar":

Bulbs broke out of boxes hunting for chinks in the dark,
Shoots dangled and drooped . . .

* * * * *

Nothing would give up life:
Even the dirt kept breathing a small breath.

Then to the "Forcing House," where all the vines and shoots and flowers "pulse with the knocking pipes." And from here to the introduction of the small boy, working as "Weed Puller"

Under the concrete benches,
Hacking at black hairy roots,—

* * * * *

With everything blooming above me,
Lilies, pale-pink cyclamen, roses,
Whole fields lovely and inviolate,—
Me down in that fetor of weeds,
Crawling on all fours,
Alive, in a slippery grave.

The word "grave," at the close of this scene of primitive vigor and struggle, reminds us that death is never very far away from growth. As in any vision of pastoral innocence, the strength of the life-giving imagery cannot be felt without the constant sense of struggle against some threatening, antagonistic force. Thus in that breathing "Root Cellar" the shoots have "long yellow evil necks, like tropical snakes," and in the following poem, "Orchids," we see how these exotic blooms "lean over the path,/ Adder-mouthed,"

Swaying close to the face,
Coming out, soft and deceptive . . .

* * * * *

And at night,
The faint moon falling through whitewashed glass,
The heat going down

So their musky smell comes even stronger,
Drifting down from their mossy cradles:
So many devouring infants!
Soft luminescent fingers,
Lips neither dead nor alive,
Loose ghostly mouths
Breathing.

The beauty of growth, we see, is ambiguous: one can never escape the presence of some poisonous threat. After this evocation of danger it is appropriate that the next poem, "Moss-Gathering," should recognize the funerary function of the greenhouse and make plain the fact that a greenhouse is not nature itself, but nature sophisticated by art:

To loosen with all ten fingers held wide and limber
And lift up a patch, dark-green, the kind for lining cemetery baskets,
Thick and cushiony, like an old-fashioned door-mat,
The crumbling small hollow sticks on the underside mixed with roots,
And wintergreen berries and leaves still stuck to the top,—
That was moss-gathering.
But something always went out of me when I dug loose those carpets
Of green, or plunged to my elbows in the spongy yellowish moss of the marshes:
And afterwards I always felt mean, jogging back over the logging road,
As if I had broken the natural order of things in that swampland;
Disturbed some rhythm, old and of vast importance,
By pulling off flesh from the living planet;
As if I had committed, against the whole scheme of life, a desecration.

Those loose and open rhythms, the closely observed details of natural growth, the frank confession, the sense of a desecration —these things evoke the spirit of D. H. Lawrence, to whose works Roethke was deeply devoted in the early 1930's—another sign that his metaphysical mode of that time was superimposed upon a deeper allegiance.

The next poem, "Big Wind," as Kenneth Burke has shown in his indispensable essay on Roethke's "Vegetal Radicalism," [1] is one of the best in the volume, with its greenhouse sailing like a great ship in the storm:

> She hove into the teeth of it,
> The core and pith of that ugly storm,
> Ploughing with her stiff prow,
> Bucking into the wind-waves
> That broke over the whole of her,
> Flailing her sides with spray,
> Flinging long strings of wet across the roof-top,
> Finally veering, wearing themselves out, merely
> Whistling thinly under the wind-vents;
> She sailed into the calm morning,
> Carrying her full cargo of roses.

("*Into* the calm morning" is the original reading: "into" has become "until" in the 1958 printing of this poem, but the latter is, I hope, only a misprint, for "sailing into" is essential to the poem's dynamic, triumphant close.) "Big Wind" throws a special emphasis upon the physical properties of the greenhouse, its "manure-machine," its "steam-plant," its "rusty boiler," its "cypress window-frames"; all these details serve, like the similar images of "Forcing House," to stress the element of deliberate art in the creation of these flowers, an art now stressed more clearly in the two following poems, "Old Florist" and "Transplanting," where we see first

> That hump of a man bunching chrysanthemums
> Or pinching-back asters, or planting azaleas,
> Tamping and stamping dirt into pots,—

and then find ourselves

> Watching hands transplanting,
> Turning and tamping,

[1] *Sewanee Review*, 58 (1950), 68-108.

Lifting the young plants with two fingers,
Sifting in a palm-full of fresh loam . . .

Such art is necessary for the growth of the flower—and of the boy—the poet suggests in his delicate associative way, by leading us from the conclusion of "Transplanting" directly into a picture of the "Child on Top of a Greenhouse":

The young horns winding and unwinding,
Creaking their thin spines,
The underleaves, the smallest buds
Breaking into nakedness,
The blossoms extending
Out into the sweet air,
The whole flower extending outward,
Stretching and reaching.

The wind billowing out the seat of my britches,
My feet crackling splinters of glass and dried putty,
The half-grown chrysanthemums staring up like accusers,
Up through the streaked glass, flashing with sunlight,
A few white clouds all rushing eastward,
A line of elms plunging and tossing like horses
And everyone, everyone pointing up and shouting!

After this, "Flower-Dump" provides a subtle, ironic qualification of this victorious, exultant scene, when we read of the "beds of bloom pitched on a pile,"

Everything limp
But one tulip on top
One swaggering head
Over the dying, the newly dead.

But the sequence ends with the triumph of art in one of the most intricate of all these greenhouse growths, "Carnations," evoking

A crisp hyacinthine coolness,
Like that clear autumnal weather of eternity,
The windless perpetual morning above a September cloud.

The sequence is one of the permanent achievements of modern poetry; its poems deserve to cling to future anthologies like Marvell's "Garden" or Wordsworth's poem about the daffodils. But in Roethke's collected verse, we should note, there is an intrusion, the poem "Frau Bauman, Frau Schmidt, and Frau Schwartze," which is interposed between "Old Florist" and "Transplanting." The insertion first occurred in Roethke's volume *The Waking* (1953), where the poem is carefully starred in the table of contents as "New poem, not published in original sequence." This note has disappeared in *Words for the Wind* (1958), where we are now most likely to read the sequence. "Frau Bauman" was first published in 1952, about four years after the completion of the other poems in this series, at a time when Roethke's Yeatsian period was first strongly manifested: "I take this cadence from a man named Yeats," Roethke says in the final section of *The Waking* (in "Four for Sir John Davies"). This long period of Yeatsian imitation no doubt performed an essential function for Roethke. After the intimate self-discoveries of *The Lost Son,* some sort of mask, like the earlier mask of the metaphysicals, was apparently needed for Roethke's further development: to escape from the incoherencies of the new poems that appeared in *Praise to the End* (1951), to include a larger measure of intellectual content, and to achieve a broader symbolic dimension. How this influence worked we can see well in "Frau Bauman":

> Gone the three ancient ladies
> Who creaked on the greenhouse ladders,
> Reaching up white strings
> To wind, to wind
> The sweet-pea tendrils, the smilax. . . .

The three workers are like Fates, winding the tendrils around the white strings. This kind of allusion, along with the formal inversion of the opening line, indicates a departure from the natural idiom and the localized greenhouse imagery of the original sequence. That departure accords with the distance that this new poem places between the child and the adult, by an overt description of the sadness of the adult state, and also by a careful literary echo of Yeats's poem "The Magi":

I remember how they picked me up, a spindly kid,
Pinching and poking my thin ribs
Till I lay in their laps, laughing,
Weak as a whiffet;
Now, when I'm alone and cold in my bed,
They still hover over me,
These ancient leathery crones,
With their bandannas stiffened with sweat,
And their thorn-bitten wrists,
And their snuff-laden breath blowing lightly over me in my first sleep.

The echo is well-handled, with an effect of wry humor, and the whole poem is finely done, in its way; but it breaks the natural, intimate presence of those earlier poems, and it ought to be printed elsewhere in future editions of Roethke's poetry.

Indeed the whole volume, *The Lost Son*, ought to be read in its first integrity, which Roethke began to alter in *Praise to the End* (1951). There the four long poems that conclude *The Lost Son* appear as the first four in a sequence of seven poems (later enlarged to eight in *The Waking*). This longer sequence is preceded in *Praise to the End* by a new and highly experimental sequence which evidently attempts to create a surrealist ground of the subconscious from which the other sequence can develop. The new effect is in itself interesting, although the new poems of *Praise to the End* too often destroy themselves by violent experiments in a Tom o' Bedlam style. Moreover, it is a serious loss to have the final poems of *The Lost Son* separated from the greenhouse sequence, which they echo and complete.

In *The Lost Son*, after those poems of the greenhouse Eden (Kenneth Burke cites Roethke as speaking of "the greenhouse— my symbol for the whole of life, a womb, a heaven-on-earth"),

Roethke has placed two brief sections containing a dozen poems that are miscellaneous in their subject matter, but not in their arrangement. Part II of the volume opens with a childhood romp with a somewhat tipsy father, moves to the sixteen-year-old working in the pickle factory, then to the adult, slave to offices, and overwhelmed by

> the inexorable sadness of pencils,
> Neat in their boxes, dolor of pad and paper-weight,
> All the misery of manila folders and mucilage . . .

and from there to other poems of desolation, including the powerful presentation of mental breakdown in a perfect poem, "The Return":

> A cold key let me in
> That self-infected lair;
> And I lay down with my life,
> With the rags and rotting clothes,
> With a stump of scraggy fang
> Bared for a hunter's boot.

Part III narrates a gradual recovery, slowly built up from an apprehension of "that cold, granitic slime" and from a remarkable tribute to the tenacious life and healing power of the smallest creatures, in "The Minimal":

> Squirmers in bogs,
> And bacterial creepers
> Wriggling through wounds
> Like elvers in ponds,
> Their wan mouths kissing the warm sutures,
> Cleaning and caressing,
> Creeping and healing.

Lastly, part IV of *The Lost Son* is comprised of Roethke's first sequence of longer poems, "The Lost Son," "The Long Alley," "A Field of Light," and "The Shape of the Fire." Kenneth Burke has analysed these poems in admirable detail; what I should like to add here is twofold. First, an impression of the meditative action in these poems, foreshadowing the associative technique of the new "North American Sequence"; and secondly, a view of the ways in which these poems complete and unify the whole volume, *The Lost Son.*

These four poems all work in the same general way, especially the first, second, and fourth, which are composed in five parts, with the last two parts representing the movement of the mind out of chaos into the light. The third poem, however, is composed in only three parts, and offers within itself a view of the development of the entire sequence. The method of exploration followed in all these poems is basically the same as that found in "Meditation at Oyster River." It consists of arousing, first, a flurry of images, as in one of those old glass spheres where we used to shake up a flurry of snowflakes and then watch them settle down around a clear landscape, or as in that poem by Frost where the speaker, watching the water in a well, sees or thinks he sees a flash of truth at the bottom. The method may be found at work within the purview of a whole sequence, or within a poem in the sequence, or within a section of a poem in the sequence. In Roethke's new volume the third section of "The Rose," for example, opens with a whirling catalogue of "American sounds," in deliberate tribute to Whitman, including everything from the bobolink to the bulldozer, but after a dozen of these mixed images, the mind at last focuses upon a central sound:

> I return to the twittering of swallows above water,
> And that sound, that single sound,
> When the mind remembers all,
> And gently the light enters the sleeping soul . . .

Thus in the final sequence of *The Lost Son,* each poem opens with a flight from ordinary "reality" into the irrational, the animal, the realm of the fish, the rat, the mouse, the cat, the eel, the otter, the mole. There are many implications of a return to the womb: "I feel the slime of a wet nest." These primitive images are given in a mode of flickering, sometimes ranting, incoherence, simulating the breakup of established modes of consciousness. Then, out of all this apparent disarray of being, there arises the strict, clear, calm imagery of that greenhouse Eden: warmth, power, growth, movement toward the light, as in the fourth section of the title poem:

> There was always a single light
> Swinging by the fire-pit,
> Where the fireman pulled out roses,
> The big roses, the big bloody clinkers.
>
> Once I stayed all night,
> The light in the morning came slowly over the white
> Snow.
> There were many kinds of cool
> Air.
> Then came steam.
>
> Pipe-knock.

(Kenneth Burke, in his comment on this poem, cites Roethke as authority for the interpretation that the "knock" is both the steam in the pipes and the knock of the father's smoking-pipe as he approaches, bringing ordered life to the scene:)

> Scurry of warm over small plants.
> Ordnung! Ordnung!
> Papa is coming!
>
> A fine haze moved off the leaves;
> Frost melted on far panes;
> The rose, the chrysanthemum turned toward the light.
> Even the hushed forms, the bent yellowy weeds
> Moved in a slow up-sway.

In each of the succeeding poems this coming of light out of the primordial darkness is stronger, steadier, more inclusive, until it brings us finally to the man of full maturity and conscious power, controlling his fate as he controls the oars of his boat. In the fourth section of "The Long Alley" (matching the fourth section of "The Lost Son") the greenhouse imagery emerges like a dream under water and becomes identified with a vital force within the human memory:

> Come, come out of the shade, the cool ways,
> The long alleys of string and stem;
> Bend down, small breathers, creepers and winders;
> Lean from the tiers and benches,
> Cyclamen dripping and lilies.
> What fish-ways you have, littlest flowers,
> Swaying over the walks, in the watery air,
> Drowsing in soft light, petals pulsing.

That word "Drowsing" is important: it relates to the "watery drowse" of the next poem here, and to the "simple drowse" of the final poem; it looks back to the first line of the entire volume:

> Sticks-in-a-drowse droop over sugary loam . . .

It suggests a dream-like state of potential regeneration, where the stems of the mind renew their vitality, as in the climax of "The Long Alley":

> Light airs! Light airs! A pierce of angels!
> The leaves, the leaves become me!
> The tendrils have me!

In "A Field of Light" the growing mind moves toward a higher state of renewed consciousness as it goes beyond the greenhouse to apprehend the unique individuality of living things:

> I touched the ground, the ground warmed by the killdeer,
> The salt laughed and the stones;
> The ferns had their ways, and the pulsing lizards,
> And the new plants, still awkward in their soil,
> The lovely diminutives.
> I could watch! I could watch!
> I saw the separateness of all things! . . .

And I walked, I walked through the light air;
I moved with the morning.

Finally, in the last two sections of "The Shape of the Fire," childhood and maturity are placed side by side in their proper dimensions, as the adult mind, knowing its powers, judges the state of childhood, with all its easy beauty, inferior to its ultimate growth. The fourth section leans backward toward the early state of the natural stem:

Morning-fair, follow me further back
Into that minnowy world of weeds and ditches . . .

That air and shine: and the flicker's loud summer call:
The bearded boards in the stream and the all of apples;
The glad hen on the hill; and the trellis humming.
Death was not. I lived in a simple drowse:
Hands and hair moved through a dream of wakening blossoms.

Yet the final section presents the power of the full growth:

To have the whole air!—
The light, the full sun
Coming down on the flowerheads . . .

And the volume ends with two powerful, summarizing images. First the image of a tranquil being, in a moment of deep thought, oars poised upon a lake for further rowing; and then the companion image of the flower's destiny: the transient perfection of the flower, set at last in its ultimate vase:

To follow the drops sliding from a lifted oar,
Held up, while the rower breathes, and the small boat drifts quietly
shoreward;
To know that light falls and fills, often without our knowing,
As an opaque vase fills to the brim from a quick pouring,
Fills and trembles at the edge yet does not flow over,
Still holding and feeding the stem of the contained flower.

Roethke never surpassed the achievement of *The Lost Son,* though many of his later poems are filled to the same brim. In these green images Roethke reached the center of his memory and found his wholly individual idiom. The "Far Field" recovered in his last volume is the same interior region reached in "A Field of Light."

X

Wallace Stevens:
The Skeptical Music

Canaries in the morning, orchestras
In the afternoon, balloons at night. That is
A difference, at least, from nightingales,
Jehovah and the great sea-worm. The air
Is not so elemental nor the earth
So near.
But the sustenance of the wilderness
Does not sustain us in the metropoles.
("Academic Discourse at Havana")

THUS Wallace Stevens represents the state of man from which his poems spring. The world of Greek myth and traditional beauty, the world of the Hebrew Deity, the world of Nordic legend—worlds of imaginative faith and of unity between man and the universe—these things are gone. No manna falls. The poet lives in a world from which the elemental, the supernatural, and the mythical have been drained, and in which the deeper instincts of the human race are consequently starving. Somehow, by his own mind and senses, man must find sustenance, must make terms with air and earth, must establish some relation between himself and the world about him. The "war between the mind/And sky, between thought and day and night," must be resolved: this is the poet's mission.

As a result, his hymn "To the One of Fictive Music" is only in part nostalgic. The echoes of the ancient litanies to the Virgin that run throughout this poem serve primarily to celebrate the redemptive power of the human imagination, the creative, nourishing power of the mind that can give transcendence and glory to familiar things:

> Sister and mother and diviner love,
> And of the sisterhood of the living dead
> Most near, most clear, and of the clearest bloom,
> And of the fragrant mothers the most dear
> And queen, and of diviner love the day
> And flame and summer and sweet fire . . .
>
> . . . of all vigils musing the obscure,
> That apprehends the most which sees and names,
> As in your name, an image that is sure,
> Among the arrant spices of the sun,
> O bough and bush and scented vine, in whom
> We give ourselves our likest issuance.
>
> Yet not too like, yet not so like to be
> Too near, too clear, saving a little to endow
> Our feigning with the strange unlike, whence springs
> The difference that heavenly pity brings.
> For this, musician, in your girdle fixed
> Bear other perfumes. On your pale head wear
> A band entwining, set with fatal stones.
> Unreal, give back to us what once you gave:
> The imagination that we spurned and crave.

This is one of Stevens' earlier poems, published in *Harmonium*, but one finds here his aesthetic and philosophy (or rather, his aesthetic-philosophy) fully developed, as perhaps one might expect in a poet who published his first volume at the age of forty-four. His later poems re-explore and restate, but do not centrally modify this view of the imagination's role in life. Over twenty years later, in *Esthétique du Mal*, one finds the same theme, now expressed in the muted, more austere tone of an older man who has mastered a meditative, more abstract form of poetry:

> The death of Satan was a tragedy
> For the imagination. A capital
> Negation destroyed him in his tenement
> And, with him, many blue phenomena.

Blue, as in Stevens' sequence "The Man with the Blue Guitar," is a symbol of the imagination. Without that dominant, sustaining blue:

> How cold the vacancy
> When the phantoms are gone and the shaken realist
> First sees reality. The mortal no
> Has its emptiness and tragic expirations.
> The tragedy, however, may have begun,
> Again, in the imagination's new beginning,
> In the yes of the realist spoken because he must
> Say yes, spoken because under every no
> Lay a passion for yes that had never been broken.

The history of man, like the histories of individual men, is a series of tragic dramas decreed by the fact of mortality, by "the unalterable necessity/Of being this unalterable animal." But what is this "yes of the realist" that may, perhaps, mark the beginning of another drama? It must be some affirmation that can achieve what Stevens in *Harmonium* has called

> The liaison, the blissful liaison,
> Between himself and his environment,
> Which was, and is, chief motive, first delight,
> For him, and not for him alone.

Whether expressed in the splendor and gaudiness of *Harmonium* or in the more restrained verse of his later volumes, the answer is the same. It lies in the cultivation of sensibility and in the affirmation of that sensibility through works of the human imagination.

We may see clearly the early action of that affirmation in the poem "Nomad Exquisite" from *Harmonium:*

As the immense dew of Florida
Brings forth
The big-finned palm
And green vine angering for life,

As the immense dew of Florida
Brings forth hymn and hymn
From the beholder,
Beholding all these green sides
And gold sides of green sides,

And blessed mornings,
Meet for the eye of the young alligator,
And lightning colors
So, in me, come flinging
Forms, flames, and the flakes of flames.

The speaker has established a liaison with nature: the dew of Florida makes him too a green thing "angering for life"; the world is a unity; man lives and grows, as the poem itself achieves unity and growth by its subtle repetitions and balances, and by its binding, emphatic sound-effects, coming to a bold climax in the final line. It is interesting to compare this with Stevens' view of a sunrise presented more than twenty years later, in the poem entitled simply "The Red Fern":

The large-leaved day grows rapidly,
And opens in this familiar spot
Its unfamiliar, difficult fern,
Pushing and pushing red after red.

There are doubles of this fern in clouds,
Less firm than the paternal flame,
Yet drenched with its identity,
Reflections and off-shoots, mimic-motes

And mist-mites, dangling seconds, grown
Beyond relation to the parent trunk:
The dazzling, bulging, brightest core,
The furiously burning father-fire . . .

Infant, it is enough in life
To speak of what you see. But wait
Until sight wakens the sleepy eye
And pierces the physical fix of things.

Here again, in more restrained style, though with the same high subtleties of sound, we have a picture of a world in order: sun, land, and cloud in a unity realized through the eye of man. But not beheld by the simple physical eye—the eye of the imagination has formed this vision in a single dominant image, which rises through a delicate harmony of sound-effects to the climactic third stanza, and closes with a meditative simplicity typical of the later Stevens.

Amid this "moving chaos that never ends," order is thus found by the poet in moments of supreme awareness, when one object, one scene, one person, one idea, is firmly grasped by integrated mind and sense. Round that one thing the world composes itself, relation is established, as in "Woman Looking at a Vase of Flowers":

the inhuman colors fell
Into place beside her, where she was,
Like human conciliations, more like
A profounder reconciling, an act,
An affirmation free from doubt.
The crude and jealous formlessness
Became the form and the fragrance of things
Without clairvoyance, close to her.

The affirmation is the momentary experience of unity and stability. This sense of the "completed scene" will not last, but for a time things are

Placed, so, beyond the compass of change,
Perceived in a final atmosphere;

For a moment final . . .

These experiences may be simple perceptions of the "rankest trivia," which Stevens (referring to his Crispin) calls "tests of the strength/Of his aesthetic, his philosophy"; they may be the realization of large, complex landscapes; they may be explorations into the realm of the pure idea. It is important to be clear about this last point, for Stevens has been called a hater of ideas and of reason. Though some of his less guarded exclamations may seem to bear this out, *Notes Toward a Supreme Fiction* should dispel any misconception. His apparent hatred of reason is at bottom only a hatred of what he calls "reason's click-clack, its applied/Enflashings." The practical, systematic application of rational power destroys imagination, limits sensibility, crushes men into "The Common Life": "A black line beside a white line," a place where "The men have no shadows / And the women have only one side."

> Rationalists, wearing square hats,
> Think, in square rooms,
> Looking at the floor,
> Looking at the ceiling,

missing the significant landscapes. But his "major man," poet, prophet, philosopher, or all three in one, comes

> from reason,
> Lighted at midnight by the studious eye,
> Swaddled in revery . . .

This speculative reason, "This warmth in the blood-world for the pure idea," stirs his admiration, for reason striving to conceive the Platonic Idea is a fictive power.

Such a union of poetry and philosophy is declared in the later poem "Asides on the Oboe," but had already been implied in the early "Homunculus et la Belle Étoile," where he says of the starlight:

> It is a good light, then, for those
> That know the ultimate Plato,
> Tranquillizing with this jewel
> The torments of confusion.

Notes Toward a Supreme Fiction sums it all up:

> The poem refreshes life so that we share,
> For a moment, the first idea . . . It satisfies
> Belief in an immaculate beginning
>
> And sends us, winged by an unconscious will,
> To an immaculate end. We move between these points:
> From that ever-early candor to its late plural
>
> And the candor of them is the strong exhilaration
> Of what we feel from what we think, of thought
> Beating in the heart, as if blood newly came,
>
> An elixir, an excitation, a pure power.
> The poem, through candor, brings back a power again
> That gives a candid kind to everything.

Candor, in its root meaning, here signifies the thing grasped in its radiant essence, the full, clear, white, pure, dazzling realization of the world and all things in it. The "ever-early candor" is the original idea of the thing, or the thing as it should be; "its late plural" is the varied manifestation of that essence as now exhibited in the world about us—often a sorry assortment of objects encrusted with the dirt of time, but, seen in their first idea, radiant. Then "Life's nonsense pierces us with strange relation," and the imagination has, for the moment, achieved its constant function, for "The first idea is an imagined thing."

Such perceptions are hardly to be planned, but they come to the man who trains his imagination to perceive them. Perhaps, says Stevens,

> The truth depends on a walk around a lake,
>
> A composing as the body tires, a stop
> To see hepatica, a stop to watch
> A definition growing certain and
>
> A wait within that certainty, a rest
> In the swags of pine-trees bordering the lake.

Note here the interaction of precise generality and precise concreteness, each supporting and enriching the other, as if the abstract definition were a flower or a grove. And indeed it is: the flower, the grove, perceived in candor, define momentarily the observer's place in the world. It is a delicate and complicated skill, this realization of candor:

> . . . the difficultest rigor is forthwith,
> On the image of what we see, to catch from that
>
> Irrational moment its unreasoning . . .

Then,

> We reason of these things with later reason
> And we make of what we see, what we see clearly
> And have seen, a place dependent on ourselves.

But modern man is too often subordinate to the place, defeated by his environment. *Notes Toward a Supreme Fiction* dramatizes this failure by contrast with the animal kingdom:

> The lion roars at the enraging desert,
> Reddens the sand with his red-colored noise,
> Defies red emptiness to evolve his match,
>
> Master by foot and jaws and by the mane,
> Most supple challenger.

Red, symbol of anger and violent blood, dominates and fills the emptiness of inanimate nature. And similarly,

> the elephant
> Breaches the darkness of Ceylon with blares,
>
> The glitter-goes on surfaces of tanks,
> Shattering velvetest far-away. The bear,
> The ponderous cinnamon, snarls in his mountain
>
> At summer thunder and sleeps through winter snow.
> But you, ephebe, look from your attic window,
> Your mansard with a rented piano. You lie

In silence upon your bed. You clutch the corner
Of the pillow in your hand. You writhe and press
A bitter utterance from your writhing, dumb,

Yet voluble of dumb violence. You look
Across the roofs as sigil and as ward
And in your centre mark them and are cowed . . .

These are the heroic children whom time breeds
Against the first idea—to lash the lion,
Caparison elephants, teach bears to juggle.

The piano, along with other musical instruments, is used by Stevens as a symbol of the imagination: in this context "rented piano" is both literally right and symbolically an exact expression of decayed imagination. The roofs form a *sigil*—a seal, an enchanting talisman; or a *ward*—a guard, a prison; both words also suggest a legal bond. In such bondage the prime function, the very idea of man, has been lost: man is not alive unless he can achieve the creative power and "human arrangement" implied by the circus imagery of the final lines.

Only the imagination can achieve this desired freedom and domination, as the singing woman beside the sea creates "The Idea of Order at Key West." "The ever-hooded, tragic-gestured sea" is used by Stevens, early and late, to represent "The World without Imagination," the "universal machine":

The water never formed to mind or voice,
Like a body wholly body, fluttering
Its empty sleeves; and yet its mimic motion
Made constant cry, caused constantly a cry,
That was not ours although we understood,
Inhuman, of the veritable ocean.

But as the woman at Key West sings, the sea becomes a part of her song; she creates, she composes the scene:

It may be that in all her phrases stirred
The grinding water and the gasping wind;
But it was she and not the sea we heard.

For she was the maker of the song she sang . . .

It was her voice that made
The sky acutest at its vanishing.
She measured to the hour its solitude.
She was the single artificer of the world
In which she sang. And when she sang, the sea,
Whatever self it had, became the self
That was her song, for she was the maker. Then we,
As we beheld her striding there alone,
Knew that there never was a world for her
Except the one she sang, and, singing, made.

And as the listeners leave the spot, it seems that "The lights in the fishing boats at anchor there"

Mastered the night and portioned out the sea,
Fixing emblazoned zones and fiery poles,
Arranging, deepening, enchanting night.

The unique vision of Stevens may be illustrated by comparing this poem with one by Wordsworth that may have suggested it: "The Solitary Reaper." In Wordsworth's poem the imagery draws the reader away from the scene and the figure of the singer during the two central stanzas: the poet's main effort is bent toward moving outward by connotation from the particular Highland girl and spot into the breadth of the world and the depth of history. The girl's song suggests immense distances of space and time. This is, no doubt, the peculiar greatness of nineteenth-century romantic poetry at its best. But in Stevens' poem the whole effort is bent toward realizing the particular spot and figure; the scene focuses inward upon the singer. So, throughout Stevens' poetry, the radiant particular is fixed in its place, for in his world it is only thus that man may dominate "The meaningless plungings of water and the wind." "Blessed rage for order," says Stevens, rage, that is, for more than the mechanical order of the sea, whose

merely revolving wheel
Returns and returns, along the dry, salt shore.
There is a mother whose children need more than that.

The human need—to realize and thus compose and dominate the world by imagination:

Poet, patting more nonsense foamed
From the sea, conceive for the courts
Of these academies, the diviner health
Disclosed in common forms. Set up
The rugged black, the image. Design
The touch. Fix quiet.

The poet, modeler of sand, pats the meaningless variety tossed up by the sea of physical life and another Venus emerges from the foam.

II

Thus, in the world of Wallace Stevens, the poet, "meaning by the poet any man of imagination," [1] attempts to work out his own salvation. The task is strenuous, for here is a fluent, glittering world, a world of eternal change, a world in which one veers from exaltation to dejection and back again, seeking the bright moments that justify man's sombre fate, seeking always

the visible rock, the audible,
The brilliant mercy of a sure repose,
On this present ground, the vividest repose,
Things certain sustaining us in certainty.

Man tires of the strenuous search, feels at times the desire to relax in a merely passive connection with the world about him, wishes at times "To have the ant of the self changed to an ox/ With its organic boomings." He tires, too, of the "exhilarations

[1] From Stevens' comment printed on the dust jacket of *The Man with the Blue Guitar and Other Poems* (New York, Alfred A. Knopf, 1937).

of changes" in an active sensibility, wishes at times to see the world "Without shadows, without magnificence,/The flesh, the bone, the dirt, the stone." Such variations are the inevitable minor of Stevens' major. Yet the dominant tone is sure and clear: the "central" of the mind is action, creation; thus in "Hibiscus on the Sleeping Shores" the mind is imaged as a moth:

> that monstered moth
> Which had lain folded against the blue
> And the colored purple of the lazy sea,
>
> And which had drowsed along the bony shores,
> Shut to the blather that the water made,
> Rose up besprent and sought the flaming red
>
> Dabbled with yellow pollen.

This flaming red hibiscus is an absolute, a fixity, like the ripe pear with which "autumn beguiles the fatalist," or the chrysanthemums whose fragrance disguises "the clanking mechanism/ Of machine within machine within machine," or like the lilacs from which "we breathe/An odor evoking nothing, absolute."

Such moments represent "The poem of the mind in the act of finding/What will suffice." Sometimes the mind, that roaming moth, is satisfied by a simple stillness and single clarity which reprieves it from its struggle to attain "the complicate, the amassing harmony":

> The blue woman looked and from her window named
>
> The corals of the dogwood, cold and clear,
> Cold, coldly delineating, being real,
> Clear and, except for the eye, without intrusion.

Such a satisfaction may seem far removed from the complex vision of Key West, yet one inevitably involves the other. The imagination grips the object tightly; then, as Stevens has said in a prose essay, "The proliferation of resemblances extends an object." "What our eyes behold may well be the text of life but one's meditations on the text and the disclosures of these meditations are no less a part of the structure of reality." [2] Through metaphor, even through such a simple metaphor as "corals of the dogwood," the imagination achieves a pleasurable metamorphosis of the object which "enhances the sense of reality, heightens it, intensifies it." Whether we are dealing with a simple object seen in its "first idea" or with some more complex transfiguration of that object, we are always looking with the mind's eye:

> The magnificent cause of being,
> The imagination, the one reality
> In this imagined world . . .

That is why objects do not exist apart from us: we are the makers of reality, and the "unreal" fabrications of the mind, simple or complex, are in the end our only absolutes:

> These trees and their argentines, their dark-spiced branches,
> Grow out of the spirit or they are fantastic dust.
>
> The bud of the apple is desire, the down-falling gold,
> The catbird's gobble in the morning half-awake——
>
> These are real only if I make them so. Whistle
> For me, grow green for me and, as you whistle and grow green,
>
> Intangible arrows quiver and stick in the skin
> And I taste at the root of the tongue the unreal of what is real.

For Stevens nothing will suffice but this satisfaction of continually renewing, by imaginative metamorphosis, his relation to the world of physical objects. For him, "The greatest poverty is not to live/In a physical world":

[2] "Three Academic Pieces," in *The Necessary Angel* (New York, Alfred A. Knopf, 1951), pp. 76-8.

> To lose sensibility, to see what one sees,
> As if sight had not its own miraculous thrift,
> To hear only what one hears, one meaning alone,
> As if the paradise of meaning ceased
> To be paradise, it is this to be destitute.
> This is the sky divested of its fountains.

This intense belief in the ultimate significance of acute and multifold perception gives the poetry of Wallace Stevens its unique quality. "A passionately niggling nightingale," he aims "to make a new intelligence prevail" through sure yet flexible management of precarious cadences, through deft placing of sound-effects, and through a knack for putting the unusual word in exactly the spot where it will carry the greatest meaning—often multiple meaning. Take "miraculous thrift" in the last passage. "Thrift" is saving, salvation, through a hoarding up of the few joys available to man; the word may also suggest "prosperity," "vigorous growth," and "means of thriving." Or consider the lines that follow the above passage from *Esthétique du Mal:*

> Here in the west indifferent crickets chant
> Through our indifferent crises. Yet we require
> Another chant, an incantation, as in
> Another and later genesis, music
> That buffets the shapes of its possible halcyon
> Against the haggardie.

"Indifferent crickets" include the would-be poets, the jabberers of our time; but note the multiple meaning of "indifferent" here. These voices are apathetic, not really concerned with the problems of the time; in Webster's terms, they are "neutral; neither good nor bad, large nor small, desirable nor undesirable"; they have "no preponderating influence or value." And the daily "crises" of our Western world are the same. "Haggardie" seems to be one of Stevens' numerous coinages, but its meaning is vigorously clear. It signifies the sum of things haggard: things wild, untrained, untamed, or wild-looking from "want of rest, fatigue, anxiety, terror, or worry." What we need is to be born again, new Adams, in a "paradise of meaning"; we need a creative imagination to "buffet" the "haggardie" with fictive "shapes" that will achieve some moments of man-made calm. The similarity in sound and cadence in the words "halcyon" and "haggardie" serves to emphasize the contrast between the implications of "halcyon," the fabled bird that calms the wind and waves, and "haggard," the wild hawk. Every word in the passage is thus precisely placed to carry precise meaning.

Many of the passages quoted earlier will provide similarly rich examples of the unusual word: the "green vine *angering* for life"; "a *capital* negation"; "the *arrant* spices of the sun"; "the physical *fix* of things"; "that ever-early *candor*"; "the *swags* of pine trees"; "the *glitter-goes* on surfaces of *tanks*" (the latter the exact word for the Indian setting); "the *blather* that the water made." But let us take one final example for close analysis, the first stanza of the finest poem in *Harmonium,* "Sunday Morning":

> Complacencies of the peignoir, and late
> Coffee and oranges in a sunny chair,
> And the green freedom of a cockatoo
> Upon a rug mingle to dissipate
> The holy hush of ancient sacrifice.
> She dreams a little, and she feels the dark
> Encroachment of that old catastrophe,
> As a calm darkens among water-lights.
> The pungent oranges and bright, green wings
> Seem things in some procession of the dead,
> Winding across wide water, without sound.
> The day is like wide water, without sound,
> Stilled for the passing of her dreaming feet
> Over the seas, to silent Palestine,
> Dominion of the blood and sepulchre.

"Complacencies"—the satisfactions and contentments of the physical, as with this woman who has risen "late" on a holiday, and now sits in the sun, wearing her "peignoir," the "loose dressing-gown worn while hair is combed or on coming out of bath." The French word suggests a cultured atmosphere; in every connotation it is exactly right to set this scene. Note how the abstract and foreign wording of "Complacencies of the peignoir" is at once brought to earth by the plain "Coffee and oranges"; this combination of "the imagination's Latin with/ The lingua franca et jocundissima" is one of Stevens' prime traits. "Green freedom of a cockatoo"—the green bird is out of his cage, enjoying the refreshment of freedom, like the woman herself, on this day escaping the confinements of the weekday world. These satisfactions have for her a pungency that seems to dissipate memories of the Crucifixion, or of the ritual that now, on this morning, celebrates that "ancient sacrifice." And yet she cannot quite escape these religious memories. They do not at once deeply affect her—the memories are like the dark surfaces of a calm sea. Yet, gradually, as her religious instinct asserts itself, the physical satisfactions grow pale: they "Seem things in some procession of the dead," as she remembers they are doomed to extinction. The water imagery, introduced to suggest her undulating calm of mind, now is easily transformed into an image suggesting the emptiness of a merely physical universe—and then is again transformed into the actual seas that separate her Western world from Palestine. By subtle transitions, without any break in the flow of association, we have been moved from the "complacencies" of the physical to a world of religious blood and death. Religious feeling has overwhelmed the sensory, and the earlier "complacency" seems now only the illusion of security. This is the highest achievement of what we might call the "hieratic" style of the earlier Stevens, but it is not superior to the later style of *Esthétique du Mal*. The modes of writing are different, each excellent in its kind, showing the gradual mutation in style that marks every writer whose concern for style arises from his concern with the fundamental problems of existence.

Such examples should warn us against accepting the charges of imprecision that are sometimes leveled against Stevens. Like every other poet, he has written badly at times, but his weaknesses should not blind us to his strength, which lies in the writing of "accurate songs," in what he has called "the romance of the precise." "Candor," the sole "miraculous thrift," resides for him in the precise poetic word, in "Virgilian cadences." That is why he is not merely the poetic dandy that he has been called. His interest in the precisions of poetic technique arises from his dedication to the mission of the poet in the modern world. His poems exist, as he has said in reference to *Owl's Clover*, "for the purpose of seizing and stating what makes life intelligible and desirable in the midst of great change and great confusion." [3]

> There is order in neither sea nor sun.
> The shapes have lost their glistening.
> There are these sudden mobs of men,
>
> These sudden clouds of faces and arms,
> An immense suppression, freed,
> These voices crying without knowing for what,
>
> Except to be happy, without knowing how,
> Imposing forms they cannot describe,
> Requiring order beyond their speech. . . .
>
> Some harmonious skeptic soon in a skeptical music
>
> Will unite these figures of men and their shapes
> Will glisten again with motion, the music
> Will be motion and full of shadows.

[3] From the dust jacket of *The Man with the Blue Guitar*, 1937.

The big-finned palm
And green vine angering for life,

* * * * *

So, in me, come flinging
Forms, flames, and the flakes of flames.

"The World as Meditation," on the other hand, finds its central proposition, not in any text from the surface of things, but in certain words of a human composer, Georges Enesco: "J'ai passé trop de temps à travailler mon violon, à voyager. Mais l'exercice essentiel du compositeur—la méditation—rien ne l'a jamais suspendu en moi. . . . Je vis un rêve permanent, qui ne s'arrête ni nuit ni jour." With those words as epigraph, the poem presents as its symbol of human achievement the figure of Penelope, awaiting the return of Ulysses. As the sun rises she awakens to the meditation that has composed her life:

A form of fire approaches the cretonnes of Penelope,
Whose mere savage presence awakens the world in which she
dwells.

She has composed, so long, a self with which to welcome him,
Companion to his self for her, which she imagined,
Two in a deep-founded sheltering, friend and dear friend.

* * * * *

But was it Ulysses? Or was it only the warmth of the sun
On her pillow? The thought kept beating in her like her heart.
The two kept beating together. It was only day.

It was Ulysses and it was not. Yet they had met,
Friend and dear friend and a planet's encouragement.
The barbarous strength within her would never fail.

There is, we see, a "savage presence" outside her, the primitive force of the sun, which arouses within her a "barbarous strength," some primitive human power that makes it possible for her to compose a self, with the sun's encouragement; and so she dwells in a world of belief created by her will. This sounds like the conception found at the close of Stevens' essay "The Noble Rider" (1942), where he mentions a certain nobility of mind that constitutes "a violence from within that protects us from a violence without. It is the imagination pressing back against the pressure of reality." Thus the violence of the sun might have aroused Penelope to the violent, ugly pressure of those outward suitors; but her imagination of Ulysses, her constant meditation of reunion with the man she constantly creates in her mind, this power presses back, composes within herself a world of value and order. Thus, as Stevens concludes in that essay, imagination "seems, in the last analysis, to have something to do with our self-preservation." [2]

I have used two terms, both prominent in Stevens' writings: *imagination, meditation*; they are not synonymous. Meditation is the essential exercise which, constantly practiced, brings the imagination into play, releases creative power, enables the human being to compose a sensitive, intelligent, and generous self. It is the sort of self that Stevens has found fully represented in the person of George Santayana, as he points out in an essay of 1948. "Most men's lives," he regretfully concedes, "are thrust upon them" by the outward violence; but, he insists:

> There can be lives, nevertheless, which exist by the deliberate choice of those that live them. To use a single illustration: it may be assumed that the life of Professor Santayana is a life in which the function of the imagination has had a function similar to its function in any deliberate work of art or letters. We have only to think of this present phase of it, in which, in his old age, he dwells in the head of the world, in the company of devoted women, in their convent, and in the company of familiar saints, whose presence does so much to make any convent an appropriate refuge for a generous and human philosopher. (NA, 147-8)

[2] *The Necessary Angel* (New York, Alfred A. Knopf, 1951), p. 36; cited hereafter as NA.

And so in his late poem "To an Old Philosopher in Rome" (1952) he finds the fulfillment of human existence in Santayana's reconciliation of flesh and spirit on the threshold of death:

> The sounds drift in. The buildings are remembered.
> The life of the city never lets go, nor do you
> Ever want it to. It is part of the life in your room.
> Its domes are the architecture of your bed.
>
> * * * * *
>
> It is a kind of total grandeur at the end,
> With every visible thing enlarged and yet
> No more than a bed, a chair and moving nuns,
> The immensest theatre, the pillared porch,
> The book and candle in your ambered room,
>
> Total grandeur of a total edifice,
> Chosen by an inquisitor of structures
> For himself. He stops upon this threshold,
> As if the design of all his words takes form
> And frame from thinking and is realized.

Such admiration for the power of *thinking,* for the constructive power of deliberate choice—this is not the sort of values that were being attributed to Stevens fifteen or twenty years ago. The central impact of Stevens' poetry up to about 1940 has been, I think, admirably summed up by Yvor Winters in his famous essay "Wallace Stevens or The Hedonist's Progress." There Winters, basing his thesis primarily on *Harmonium,* saw in Stevens the cultivation of "the realm of emotion divorced from understanding," the commendation of "the emotions as a good in themselves." It was, he felt, a point of view that had led Stevens from the great poetry of *Harmonium* into a "rapid and tragic decay" of style, the sad, inevitable progress of the hedonist, "unable to think himself out of the situation into which he has wandered." [3]

Winters has made a brilliant diagnosis of the malady; but he underestimated the patient's will to live. Looking back now, with the immense advantage of all that Stevens has published since Winters wrote, and with the equally great advantage of the *Opus Posthumous*—looking back now, we can see that something quite different happened. We can see something analogous to the course of Yeats's poetry. We can see a poet, by a deliberate process of self-knowledge, rebuilding himself and his poetry, rebuilding himself through his poetry, and achieving, in *Transport to Summer* (1947), a volume of meditative poetry that is in every way the equal of his great, first volume of hedonist poetry. There is of course no sudden, arbitrary change; the career of Stevens is consistent and continuous; what happens, I think, is that recessive elements in the early poetry develop gradually into dominance.

Let us try to sketch, now, this different progress. Stevens' second volume, *Ideas of Order*, appeared in 1935; its slimness, its dominant tone, and its title are all significant of a change in the poet's outlook. The buoyancy that gave forth the bounty of *Harmonium* is gone; that force within, like "the immense dew of Florida," that had brought forth "Forms, flames, and the flakes of flames" is subsiding, although here and there it reappears, the old gay defiance of Winters:

> But what are radiant reason and radiant will
> To warblings early in the hilarious trees
> Of summer, the drunken mother?

Or:

> What is there here but weather, what spirit
> Have I except it comes from the sun?

[3] *The Anatomy of Nonsense* (Norfolk, Conn., New Directions, 1943), pp. 89, 91, 97.

XI

Wallace Stevens: The World as Meditation

"IN an age of disbelief," says Wallace Stevens in a late essay, "it is for the poet to supply the satisfactions of belief, in his measure and in his style." It is my purpose here to explore the nature of those satisfactions, to examine the measure and the style that Stevens achieved in his later poetry, and in this way to suggest the answer that Stevens found to his own blunt question: "What, then, is the nature of poetry in a time of disbelief?"[1]

The answer is implicit in the late poem that provides my theme and title here: "The World as Meditation" (1952) seems to sum up the poetical discoveries of Stevens since that time, some thirty years earlier, when his Paltry Nude started on her Spring Voyage through the world of *Harmonium*, to become at the close of that volume a complete Nomad Exquisite, fully attuned to the harmonies of nature, creating as nature herself creates:

As the immense dew of Florida
Brings forth

[1] "Two or Three Ideas" (1951), in *Opus Posthumous*, ed. Samuel French Morse (New York, Alfred A. Knopf, 1957), pp. 206, 211; cited hereafter as OP.

The trouble is that the younger Nomad Exquisite had lived by a view that the poet of the 1930's could no longer accept, for reasons he suggests in the late essay cited at the outset of this discussion: "If in the minds of men creativeness was the same thing as creation in the natural world, if a spiritual planet matched the sun, or if without any question of a spiritual planet, the light and warmth of spring revitalized all our faculties, as in a measure they do, all the bearings one takes, all the propositions one formulates would be within the scope of that particular domination"—as they were, for the most part, in *Harmonium*. "The trouble is, however, that men in general do not create in light and warmth alone," he continues. "They create in darkness and coldness. They create when they are hopeless, in the midst of antagonisms, when they are wrong, when their powers are no longer subject to their control. They create as the ministers of evil" (OP, 210). *Ideas of Order* moves in this different world; it is filled with the tones of evening: "A Fading of the Sun," "Gray Stones and Gray Pigeons," "Autumn Refrain," "Winter Bells," "Sad Strains of a Gay Waltz."

> There is order in neither sea nor sun.
> The shapes have lost their glistening.
> There are these sudden mobs of men.

In this new atmosphere one poem stands out to control the chaos: the famous "Idea of Order at Key West." Here the speaker, significantly, stands at the far edge of Florida, his back upon that world of flame and green. The physical world now offers none of its old "comforts of the sun," but exists here as

> The meaningless plungings of water and the wind,
> Theatrical distances, bronze shadows heaped
> On high horizons, mountainous atmospheres
> Of sky and sea.

The object of wonder and admiration is now a human figure, that singer by the shore whose voice made

> The sky acutest at its vanishing.
> She measured to the hour its solitude.
> She was the single artificer of the world
> In which she sang.

This is more than the Palace of Hoon, the solipsist of *Harmonium;* for the idea of order here resides in more than mental landscapes, in "More even than her voice, and ours": the idea of order is found in a unique conjunction of landscape, singer, and listener, a situation in which the listener's mind, exulting in the full strength of its powers, is able to assert the controlling force of consciousness, "Fixing emblazoned zones and fiery poles" upon the outer atmosphere, "Arranging, deepening, enchanting night"—while realizing fully that the outer universe goes its inhuman way.

The fierce strength of mind in that poem, its clipped and muted language before the final exultation, prepares the way for a striking addition to the volume *Ideas of Order*, when it appeared in a trade edition in the next year, 1936. The volume no longer opens with the curiously fatigued poem, "Sailing After Lunch," where Stevens truly says, "My old boat goes round on a crutch / And doesn't get under way," and where he ends with the sentimental desire

> To expunge all people and be a pupil
> Of the gorgeous wheel and so to give
> That slight transcendence to the dirty sail.

No, the volume now opens with the stirring "Farewell to Florida," in which Stevens renounces all that "Florida" has symbolized in his earlier poetry: that world of vivid physical apprehension, where man created within the bounds of the natural order. "Her mind had bound me round," he says, but now he cries:

> Go on, high ship, since now, upon the shore,
> The snake has left its skin upon the floor.

> Key West sank downward under massive clouds
> And silvers and greens spread over the sea. The moon
> Is at the mast-head and the past is dead.
> Her mind will never speak to me again.

And he looks forward to his engagement with a new, a tough, bitter, and turbulent subject:

> My North is leafless and lies in a wintry slime
> Both of men and clouds, a slime of men in crowds.
> The men are moving as the water moves,
> This darkened water cloven by sullen swells
> Against your sides, then shoving and slithering,
> The darkness shattered, turbulent with foam.
> To be free again, to return to the violent mind
> That is their mind, these men, and that will bind
> Me round, carry me, misty deck, carry me
> To the cold, go on, high ship, go on, plunge on.

Stevens, it is clear, has determined to take his old boat out of "The Pleasures of Merely Circulating," to plunge into the turmoil of the mid-thirties, to engage it somehow in his poetry. In fact, he had already begun the effort. The year before "Farewell to Florida" appeared he had already published the first part of what was to become his longest poetical effort, *Owl's Clover,* which appeared in 1936 in its original version of 861 lines. It is a poem that caused Stevens immense labor and, finally, intense dissatisfaction. In 1937 it reappeared with nearly 200 lines cut out; and in 1954 Stevens omitted it entirely from his *Collected Poems,* on the grounds that it was "rhetorical," Mr. Morse tells us (OP, xxiii). As a result of this drastic omission, the reader of the *Collected Poems* may emerge with a sense of the poet's steady self-possession—an ideal progress from the old gaudy style toward a sober, muted, thoughtful, pruned, and thoroughly remade poetry—for we move from *Ideas of Order* directly into "The Man with the Blue Guitar," where

> The man bent over his guitar,
> A shearsman of sorts.

A shearsman indeed, a sort of tailor, cutting his cloth anew and shearing away the excess.[4] But the effect is too neat. We need *Owl's Clover*, preferably in its first version, to tell us all the trouble of the change; and fortunately we have it all now before us once again, in the new posthumous volume. It is not a successful poem, though it contains great passages and opens remarkably well, with the firmly controlled symbols of "The Old Woman and the Statue." There the magnificent statue in the park represents the soaring, noble imagination of the past, "leaping in the storms of light": the statue is a work of art subtly and powerfully arranged for the human mind to grasp and be exalted. One thing, one thing only, the sculptor "had not foreseen": the old woman, "the bitter mind/In a flapping cloak," a woman so depressed that she cannot apprehend the statue's action:

> A woman walking in the autumn leaves,
> Thinking of heaven and earth and of herself
> And looking at the place in which she walked,
> As a place in which each thing was motionless
> Except the thing she felt but did not know.

That thing is the "harridan self," "Crying against a need that pressed like cold,/Deadly and deep." It is not simply physical poverty that tortures this suffering self: it is that she lives, as the second part tells us, amid "the immense detritus of a world"

> That is completely waste, that moves from waste
> To waste, out of the hopeless waste of the past
> Into a hopeful waste to come.

The hopeful waste of the future, I think, alludes to the sort of world proffered by Mr. Burnshaw, whose name adorns the original title of the second part: "Mr. Burnshaw and the Statue" (later altered to "The Statue at the World's End"). Stanley

[4] See Stevens' explanation of this figure in a letter to his Italian translator, Renato Poggioli: "This refers to the posture of the speaker, squatting like a tailor (a shearsman) as he works on his cloth." *Mattino Domenicale ed Altre Poesie* (Turin, 1954), p. 174.

Burnshaw was the Marxist critic who in 1935 had reviewed *Ideas of Order* with considerable acuteness, though with a condescending tone: he had seen it as a book of "speculations, questionings, contradictions"—"the record of a man who, having lost his footing, now scrambles to stand up and keep his balance." [5] The critique, being so largely true, left its mark, as *Owl's Clover* shows in its derisive rejection of all mass-solutions that offer only "an age of concentric mobs." But what can be offered instead to the suffering self? The offering in this long second section turns out, in spite of its high rhetoric, to be surprisingly meager: it is simply the old pleasures of Florida, chanted in a weak imitation of the old hieratic style of "Sunday Morning," as this passage (later removed) indicates:

> Dance, now, and with sharp voices cry, but cry
> Like damsels daubed and let your feet be bare
> To touch the grass and, as you circle, turn
> Your backs upon the vivid statue. Then,
> Weaving ring in radiant ring and quickly, fling
> Yourselves away and at a distance join
> Your hands held high and cry again, but cry,
> This time, like damsels captured by the sky,
> Seized by that possible blue.

But those waltzes had ended, long since. Clearly, the poet must try another way, and so, in his third section, Stevens turns to develop a contrast between two ways of life. One is the old way of religious meditation, where "each man,"

> Through long cloud-cloister-porches, walked alone,
> Noble within perfecting solitude,
> Like a solitude of the sun, in which the mind
> Acquired transparence and beheld itself
> And beheld the source from which transparence came.

[5] *New Masses* (Oct. 1, 1935), p. 42. Mr. Burnshaw has reprinted this review, along with an interesting commentary, in *Sewanee Review*, 69 (1961) 355-66.

And the other is something that seems to have arisen or to be arising in place of the old religious way, something he calls Africa, a world of dense, savage, mindless animality, where

> Death, only, sits upon the serpent throne:
> Death, the herdsman of elephants,
> To whom the jaguars cry and lions roar
> Their petty dirges of fallen forest-men,
> Forever hunting or hunted, rushing through
> Endless pursuit or endlessly pursued,
> Until each tree, each evil-blossomed vine,
> Each fretful fern drops down a fear like dew.

From here on, in the middle of the poem, *Owl's Clover* provides less and less sustenance for the troubled mind trying to feed in the dark. It becomes increasingly turgid and incoherent. The old religion cannot cope with "Africa," nor can the old art of the statue; nor can the problems be met by the believers in necessity, the nostalgic admirers of the old pioneer spirit, or the worshippers of the "newest Soviet reclame." "How shall we face the edge of time?"

> Where shall we find more than derisive words?
> When shall lush chorals spiral through our fire
> And daunt that old assassin, heart's desire?

"Lush chorals"—the backward glance toward the days of *Harmonium*—is ominous, and we are not surprised to find the poem ending with a Sombre Figuration in which the poet attempts to find refuge in a vague, semi-Jungian concept of the "subman." This subman is some inner man of imagination, who lies below the torments of thought: "The man below the man below the man,/Steeped in night's opium, evading day." But the subman has a precarious tenure, for he seems to reside only in a rhetoric of empty assertion:

> And memory's lord is the lord of prophecy
> And steps forth, priestly in severity,

Yet lord, a mask of flame, the sprawling form
A wandering orb upon a path grown clear.

It is a relief to turn from this evasive subman to the daylight figure who shears away this outworn pomp. The sounds made by "The Man with the Blue Guitar" (1937) show that Stevens, within a year's hard thought, has taken quick, firm strides toward the position thoroughly established in his prose essays and his later poetry: that "the poet must get rid of the hieratic in everything that concerns him," that he must abolish "the false conception of the imagination as some incalculable *vates* within us, unhappy Rodomontade" (NA, 58, 61)—i.e. the opium-drugged subman must be erased, along with the style in which he had been expressed. In his place we will have something like Picasso's clear, clean image of the old Guitar Player, a product of his "blue period" (though the guitar itself happens to be tan), which was, incidentally, exhibited in Hartford in 1934. We will have an image of life discovered, explored, and developed through a language made out of "things exactly as they are," a language moving now with a tough intent toward the discovery of a self:

Ah, but to play man number one,
To drive the dagger in his heart,

To lay his brain upon the board
And pick the acrid colors out,

To nail his thought across the door,
Its wings spread wide to rain and snow,

To strike his living hi and ho,
To tick it, tock it, turn it true,

To bang it from a savage blue,
Jangling the metal of the strings. . . .

This is as far as we can get from the puzzled, ruminative ebb and flow of *Owl's Clover*, with its dissolving, eddying, and often turbid blank verse: note here the crisp common diction, the strict driving rhythm of the short couplets, subtly bound together by irregular rhymes and half-rhymes, all focused on one aim: a definition of the *self* as the only province of poetry:

> Ourselves in the tune as if in space,
> Yet nothing changed, except the place
>
> Of things as they are and only the place
> As you play them, on the blue guitar,
>
> Placed, so, beyond the compass of change,
> Perceived in a final atmosphere;
>
> For a moment final.

We have returned to the central position of "The Idea of Order at Key West": man's inner rage for order as the ultimate constructive force in man's universe, and hence the never-ending effort of the mind to control, within the mind, that outer monster, the inhuman universe:

> That I may reduce the monster to
> Myself, and then may be myself
>
> In face of the monster, be more than part
> Of it, more than the monstrous player of
>
> One of its monstrous lutes, not be
> Alone, but reduce the monster and be,
>
> Two things, the two together as one.

From this effort, he says, "I shall evolve a man."

This sequence of thirty-three tightly argued, tightly ordered meditations on a theme establishes the altered style of the later Stevens. He has here, in a deliberate act of choice, sheared away the kind of writing that he later calls "the romantic intoning, the declaimed clairvoyance," since this, he says, is the "appropriate idiom" of apotheosis; and this is not at all his subject now. Apotheosis elevates the mortal to the stature of divinity; it glorifies; and the appropriate poetry of apotheosis is therefore the hymn, the ode, the celebration, the chant. In a peculiar sense, this had been the appropriate idiom of his earlier poetry, since he was there attempting to show, as he tells the lady in "Sunday Morning," that "Divinity must live within" the human realm: "Passions of rain, or moods in falling snow." Hence he uses the idiom of romantic intoning to glorify the satisfactions of this earth, often with deliberate irony: the Comedian speaks of his "first central hymns, the celebrants / Of rankest trivia"; and indeed the whole mock-heroic effect of the Comedian arises from the application of such grand intoning to the achievements of this "merest minuscule."

But in his new effort to evolve a man, a new idiom must be invented, since "apotheosis is not/The origin of the major man" for whom the poet is now searching. "He comes," says Stevens, "from reason, / Lighted at midnight by the studious eye, / Swaddled in revery." He is the meditative man, master of the essential exercise, student, scholar, rabbi of a new idiom, which Stevens in "Of Modern Poetry" (1940) calls "The poem of the mind in the act of finding / What will suffice." There has never been a better definition of what might be called the genre of meditative poetry. It is not, we note, a poem celebrating what suffices; nor is it any lamentation for the lack of what suffices. The difference between the true meditative poem and other poetic genres seems to be exactly this: that it alone represents "The poem of the act of the mind," the poem of the mind, in the very act of finding. One thinks of Emily Dickinson, of Hopkins, of George Herbert, and especially of Donne, in his "Divine Meditations" (Holy Sonnets).

But further definition of the genre, if there is really such a genre, is necessary, and Stevens suggests it all in "Of Modern Poetry":

> It has to be living, to learn the speech of the place.
> It has to face the men of the time and to meet
> The women of the time. It has to think about war
> And it has to find what will suffice. It has
> To construct a new stage. It has to be on that stage
> And, like an insatiable actor, slowly and
> With meditation, speak words that in the ear,
> In the delicatest ear of the mind, repeat,
> Exactly, that which it wants to hear, at the sound
> Of which, an invisible audience listens,
> Not to the play, but to itself, expressed
> In an emotion as of two people, as of two
> Emotions becoming one.

Let me expand, with only a little liberty, the possible implications of that text. This kind of poetry must know the common speech; it must make contact with men in their normal existence, through its language, its images, and its consideration of urgent problems, such as war, of whatever kind, whether between man and man, or between body and soul, good and evil, man and his environment—the "war between the mind and sky" that Stevens describes at the end of his *Notes Toward a Supreme Fiction*. It has to find what will suffice, but in order to do this, it must construct a stage on which an actor may enact the process of this finding. And as this actor speaks his meditated words, they find a growing response in a certain invisible audience, which is not simply us, the readers or listeners, but is first of all the larger, total mind of the poet himself, controlling the actor, who is some projected aspect of himself. Then, in the close, that actor and that audience, projected self and larger self, come together in a moment of emotional resolution—for a moment final. It is a process that Stevens describes thus in his "Adagia": "When the mind is like a hall in which thought is like a voice speaking, the voice is always that of someone else." The voice is that of some projected self: the audience is the whole self. "It is necessary to propose an enigma to the mind," he says in another adage. "The mind always proposes a solution " (OP, 168). All this seems to describe something very like the action in "The Idea of Order at Key West": the landscape is the stage, the singer by the shore is the actor, and the poet's larger mind is the audience. It is also very like the action that one finds in Donne's Holy Sonnets, which we may take as a prime example of pure meditative poetry, since they seem to arise directly from the rigorous meditative exercises commonly practiced by religious men of the seventeenth century. Recall how Donne projects some aspect of himself upon a stage: the deathbed, the round earth's imagined corners, the Cross; how he then allows that self to ponder the given situation; and how, at the close, the projected self makes a subtle union with the whole mind of the poet, concluding all in the finding of what will suffice.

One can only ponder the possibilities here, and pause to stress one point. In formal religious meditation, as developed during Donne's time and later practiced (certainly) by Hopkins and (presumably) by Eliot, the process of meditation consists of something akin to that just described by Stevens. It begins with the deliberate creation of a setting and the placing there of an actor, some aspect of the self; this is the famous composition of place recommended by the Jesuit exercises. This is followed by predominantly intellectual analysis of some crucial problem pertaining to that self; and it all ends in a highly emotional resolution where the projected self and the whole mind of the meditator come together in a spirit of devotion. This threefold process is related to the old division of the soul into memory, understanding, and will; the exercise of meditation integrates these faculties.

How is it that a modern poet such as Wallace Stevens, so vastly different from the seventeenth century in the objects of his belief, should come to describe the need for a kind of poetry to which Donne's Holy Sonnets seem to belong, a kind that we might call the genre of meditative poetry? Donne's strenuous cultivation of this kind of poetry seems to be part of his lifelong effort to transcend and resolve his grievous sense of the fickleness, the dissolution, the transiency and fragility of all physical things. In Stevens, I think, an analogous situation called forth the analogous discipline. Stevens, in mid-career, recognized the dissolution, or the inadequacy, of his old poetic self—a recognition recorded with a wry gaiety in "The Comedian as the Letter C." His later poems represent a rigorous search for ways and means of evolving another kind of poetic self, in accord with the outlook expressed in the late essay dealing with the "time of disbelief": "There was always in every man the increasingly human self, which instead of remaining the observer, the nonparticipant, the delinquent, became constantly more and more all there was or so it seemed; and whether it was so or merely seemed so still left it for him to resolve life and the world in his own terms" (OP, 207).

Allusions in his prose essays indicate that in this effort Stevens engaged in broad reading among tough thinkers, while all his later poetry displays a new respect for the "radiant idea" and the "radiant will." This is clear in the first part of *Notes Toward a Supreme Fiction* (1942), which insists that the fiction must be, in some sense, "abstract." Not, I think, abstract in the usual sense of a philosophical abstraction; Stevens has told us plainly what he thinks of this in his "Landscape with Boat," where he decries the man who "wanted imperceptible air," who "wanted the eye to see"

> And not be touched by blue. He wanted to know,
> A naked man who regarded himself in the glass
> Of air, who looked for the world beneath the blue,
> Without blue, without any turquoise tint or phase,
> Any azure under-side or after-color.

By "abstract" Stevens seems rather to imply a quality of being taken out, abstracted in the root sense, from that world we call the outer universe: something concrete taken out of this and taken into the mind through a process of full, exact realization. From that "local abstraction" the turquoise tints and azure undersides can then radiate in all directions. This is the process that Stevens vividly describes in section vii of "Credences of Summer," where he begins by scorning those who have found it too hard "to sing in face/ Of the object," and have therefore fled to the woods, where they could sing "their unreal songs,/ Secure." In a violent reversal of mood, he advocates a fiercely opposite process:

> Three times the concentred self takes hold, three times
> The thrice concentred self, having possessed
>
> The object, grips it in savage scrutiny,
> Once to make captive, once to subjugate
> Or yield to subjugation, once to proclaim
> The meaning of the capture, this hard prize,
> Fully made, fully apparent, fully found.

If this bears some resemblance to the old threefold process of formal meditation, it is only because Stevens has discovered for himself the same faculties, and has taught himself a way of using them for his own meditative ends. He has, in an essay of 1943, come to define the imagination as "the sum of our faculties," and has gone on to speak of "The acute intelligence of the imagination, the illimitable resources of its memory, its power to possess the moment it perceives" (NA, 61).

Indeed, it appears that Stevens has been thoroughly aware of the analogy I am suggesting, for in a posthumously published essay, written about 1937, we find him declaring: "The poet who wishes to contemplate the good in the midst of confusion is like the mystic who wishes to contemplate God in the midst of evil. . . . Resistance to the pressure of ominous and destructive circumstance consists of its conversion, so far as possible, into a different, an explicable, an amenable circumstance." And in this search, he adds, the poets "purge themselves before reality . . . in what they intend to be saintly exercises" (OP, 225, 227).

But if we accept Stevens' use of the term *meditation* as a proper description of his own secular exercises, we may appear to be stretching the word beyond any useful signification. Cannot any poem that contains any degree of hard thinking be thus called meditative? I do not think so, if we keep in mind the careful distinctions made by the old spiritual writer François de Sales. "Every meditation is a thought," he says, "but every thought is not a meditation; for we have thoughts, to which our mind is carried without aim or design at all, by way of a simple musing. . . . And be this kind of thought as attentive as it may be, it can never bear the name of meditation." On the other hand, he says, "Sometimes we consider a thing attentively to learn its causes, effects, qualities; and this thought is named study." But "when we think of heavenly things, not to learn, but to delight in them, that is called to meditate; and the exercise thereof meditation." "So that meditation," he concludes, "is an attentive thought repeated or voluntarily maintained in the mind, to arouse the will to holy and wholesome affections and resolutions." [6]

It seems valid to adapt this definition to the meditation of earthly things, since meditation is a process, not a subject. If we do this, then Stevensian meditation becomes attentive thinking about concrete things with the aim of developing an affectionate understanding of how good it is to be alive. We can see the process working everywhere in his later poetry, but nowhere better than in "The World as Meditation," which now needs to be

[6] François de Sales, A *Treatise on the Love of God* (1616), Book vi, chap. ii; adapted from the translation of 1630.

read entire as an example of the full development of Stevens' meditative mode. Note first how far the poem's range extends beyond the "comforts of the sun": the verbal beauty of Enesco's French draws in the cosmopolitan world of the musician, as the figure of Penelope draws in the ancient world of legend. Yet the sun exists as first cause; without it there would be nothing. Thus the poem is phrased to allow a double reference: the sun is Penelope's companion, along with Ulysses. Note too how the poem fulfills all of Stevens' requirements for this modern poetry: common speech, common images, common problems; the establishment of a stage, the placing of Penelope as actor on that stage, the imputed working of her meditative thoughts, along with the constant presence of the poet's larger mind, controlling all, and concluding all with an affectionate understanding of what will suffice.

Is it Ulysses that approaches from the east,
The interminable adventurer? The trees are mended.
That winter is washed away. Someone is moving

On the horizon and lifting himself up above it.
A form of fire approaches the cretonnes of Penelope,
Whose mere savage presence awakens the world in which she
dwells.

She has composed, so long, a self with which to welcome him,
Companion to his self for her, which she imagined,
Two in a deep-founded sheltering, friend and dear friend.

The trees had been mended, as an essential exercise
In an inhuman meditation, larger than her own.
No winds like dogs watched over her at night.

She wanted nothing he could not bring her by coming alone.
She wanted no fetchings. His arms would be her necklace
And her belt, the final fortune of their desire.

But was it Ulysses? Or was it only the warmth of the sun
On her pillow? The thought kept beating in her like her heart.
The two kept beating together. It was only day.

It was Ulysses and it was not. Yet they had met,
Friend and dear friend and a planet's encouragement.
The barbarous strength within her would never fail.

She would talk a little to herself as she combed her hair,
Repeating his name with its patient syllables,
Never forgetting him that kept coming constantly so near.

The world of *Harmonium* has not been discarded here, but its reliance on the natural force of "sensibility" has been modified, and the pleasures of that world have been included within a larger structure of existence. By 1951 Stevens could strongly question "the dogma that the origins of poetry are to be found in the sensibility" and could suggest: "if one says that a fortunate poem or a fortunate painting is a synthesis of exceptional concentration . . . we find that the operative force within us does not, in fact, seem to be the sensibility, that is to say, the feelings. It seems to be a constructive faculty, that derives its energy more from the imagination than from the sensibility"—imagination being, as we have seen, the "sum of our faculties." But he adds, in his cautious way, "I have spoken of questioning, not of denying" (NA, 164). That is because the old dews of Florida have never ceased to affect him. One of his very last poems, "Prologues to What Is Possible," suggests that the value of existence may have resided in

> A flick which added to what was real and its vocabulary,
> The way some first thing coming into Northern trees
> Adds to them the whole vocabulary of the South,
> The way the earliest single light in the evening sky, in spring,
> Creates a fresh universe out of nothingness by adding itself,
> The way a look or a touch reveals its unexpected magnitudes.

There is no inconsistency here. The look, the touch, the flick of feeling, the "times of inherent excellence," "incalculable balances," "not balances / That we achieve but balances that happen"—these are things worth recognizing, and Stevens never ceases to celebrate them as part of the wonder of human consciousness. But he is quick to recognize that "the casual is not / Enough": it does not attain the full "freshness of ourselves"; it does not satisfy the "will to make iris frettings on the blank." Beyond the casual apprehensions there lie the willed and reasoned structures of the mind, which Stevens presents in two forms. One structure occurs when the mind thoroughly and fully concentrates upon the realization of some composition that appears to be inherent in the external scene, as in "Credences of Summer."

> Let's see the very thing and nothing else.
> Let's see it with the hottest fire of sight.
> Burn everything not part of it to ash.
>
> Trace the gold sun about the whitened sky
> Without evasion by a single metaphor.

Thus:

> One of the limits of reality
> Presents itself in Oley when the hay,
> Baked through long days, is piled in mows. It is
> A land too ripe for enigmas, too serene.

This seems to be what Stevens means by seeing things in their "first idea," their "ever-early candor"; this is the adequacy of landscape—for a moment final. It exists beyond us, it is no metaphor, and yet, Stevens insists, "the first idea is an imagined thing," since it is achieved by a calculated effort of the mind. It is part, then, "of the never-ending meditation," a poem of the mind in the act of finding what will suffice. It may be, he says, "of a man skating, a woman dancing, a woman / Combing," a

Woman Looking at a Vase of Flowers, a Dish of Peaches in Russia, or a Large Red Man Reading: it may be found "in the crackling summer night,"

> In the *Duft* of towns, beside a window, beside
> A lamp, in a day of the week, the time before spring,
> A manner of walking, yellow fruit, a house,
> A street.

They are acts available to any man, a sort of poetry, "an imaginative activity that diffuses itself throughout our lives" (NA, 149). You return, say, from a long vacation with your family in the mountains, dog-tired, addle-brained, and feeling the whole expedition was a huge mistake. Two weeks later, the snapshots return, developed in full color: you are amazed at the beauty, the order, the focus; the trip is a success, after all. Such a realization would be, in Stevens' terms, a poetic action.

And finally, beyond such compositions, there lies the inexhaustible "realm of resemblance," in which the faculties of the imagination, using all their powers, "extend the object" by analogy, by metaphor. It is a realm in which the whole mind, like Stevens' Penelope, uses the world of sensory experience as a base upon which to construct a total edifice involving and demanding the whole stretch of human experience. By the use of such analogies man connects the external and the internal; the action of analogy is the mind's ultimate way of establishing its dominant, controlling position amid the "moving chaos that never ends." And this, too, is an activity that Stevens sees as available to everyone.

You sit in a chair, say, admiring the beauty of your four-year-old daughter: you call to mind certain resemblances between her and her absent mother, between her and your imagined image of yourself, between her and your memories and pictures of grandparents. You think, too, of certain painted images of children by Renoir or Romney; you think of Andrew Marvell's

"Picture of Little T. C. in a Prospect of Flowers"; you think of the dogwood that bloomed last spring and of the zinnias now blooming outside. And for a moment the object toward which all these resemblances converge, or from which they infinitely extend—for a moment the object becomes a vital center through which the sense of life is composed, final: "completed in a completed scene," as Stevens says. Such is Wallace Stevens' World as Meditation, a world where the poet may adopt the words of Valéry's Architect and say, "By dint of constructing . . . I truly believe that I have constructed myself."

INDEX